Mama Prayed

Bryson Brown

© 2016 by Bryson Brown. All rights reserved.
Published by Vantage Point Publishing
Indianapolis, IN 46205

No part of this publication may be reproduced or transmitted in any form or by any means, electronic or mechanical, including photocopy, or any information storage and retrieval system, without permission from the publisher. The only exception is a brief quotation in printed reviews.

Limit of Liability/Disclaimer of Warranty: While the publisher and author have used their best efforts in preparing this book, they make no representations or warranties with respect to the accuracy or completeness of the contents of this book and specifically disclaim any implied warranties of merchantability or facilities for a particular purpose. No warranty may be created or extended by any persons. The advice or strategies herein may not be suitable for your situation. You should consult with a professional where appropriate. Neither the publisher nor author should be liable for any loss of profit or any other incidental damages, including but not limited to special, consequential, or other damages.

This is a work of fiction. Names, characters, businesses, places, events and incidents are either the products of the author's imagination or used in a fictitious manner. Any resemblance to actual persons, living or dead, or actual events is purely coincidental.

ISBN 978-1-943159-04-8

LCCN 2016911682

The publisher would appreciate notification where errors occur so that they may be corrected in subsequent printing and/or editions. Please send comments to the publisher by emailing to deeprivers67@yahoo.com

Printed in the United States of America

Dedication

This book is dedicated to my loving, late parents, Willie and Annie Brown. They laid the foundation for me to become the man that I am today. If it wasn't for their encouragement, guidance, love, support, and many life lessons, this book could not have become a reality.

I would also like to dedicate this book to my late sisters Loretta B. Canton and Brenda Brown-Bair. Their loving spirits continue to inspire me to share this gift from God.

Acknowledgments

First and foremost I would like to thank my Heavenly Father, who loved the world so much that He gave it His only begotten Son - my Lord and Savior Jesus Christ. I am truly thankful for the gifts of expression and writing that God has blessed me with and for giving me the opportunity to make this dream a reality. This second book could never have been written without the faith I have in the one true God.

To my loving wife, Dr. Sharon Y. Brown: Words cannot begin to express my appreciation for all the love, support, and spiritual guidance you have shown me over the past 25 years. I am so grateful for your editing skills and the time you have spent proofing my poems. You are truly my helpmeet and I cannot thank God enough for you. I love you more and more with each passing day.

To my children, Dominique, Janelle, Gabrielle and Bryson, Jr.: If it wasn't for you this book may have never been written. Each of you deeply inspired the writing of this book. May this book be a symbol of my love for you and an inspiration for you to reach your full potential in life and be all that God has designed you to be!

To my sister Cherry Lewis: I love you and cannot thank God enough for the best sister in the world. Thank you for always believing in me.

To my amazing family and many friends: Thank you for all of the love and support during my life. I am truly blessed to have you in my life.

A special thanks to my publisher, Dawn Blanchard, for believing in me; my brother Sterling Pettis for designing the covers for my books; and to Leevance Williams, my brother in poetry. This book would not be reality if not for your encouragement and support.

Table of Contents

1. Mama Prayed
2. Mama Was Always There
3. Motivation
4. I Believe in Love
5. Mama's Words
6. When Mama Cooked
7. I Am Who I Am
8. You Live and You Learn
9. Can We Call it the Blues?
10. Young, Gifted, and Black
11. God Gave Us Mothers
12. Hip Hop
13. No Child Left Behind
14. Katrina
15. The Masks
16. Grandma's Hands
17. Beautiful Lady
18. Darfur
19. A Generation Lost
20. Slow Reaction, No Reaction!
21. God Gave Me a Gift
22. There Is a Pulse in Haiti
23. Haiti: The Forgotten Symbol of Freedom and Strength
24. Missing
25. Mama Loved to Hug
26. Life Goes On
27. My Words Are Me
28. A Father
29. Racial Profiling: A Reality for Many
30. I Wonder...
31. My Dreams
32. The Gift of True Friendship
33. Why Would Anyone Want to Be a Nigger?

34. Daddy, Where Are You?
35. I Am
36. Every Day I Am Reminded of Me
37. No Cures
38. Mama Was a Teacher
39. Beautiful
40. How Can America Have a Problem with Immigration
41. Footprints in the Mind: An Act of Forgiveness
42. I Am Able To Smile
43. What If?
44. I Must Say Thank You
45. This Heart of Mine
46. No More Promises
47. Love and Friendship
48. Sometimes You Need to Just Get Away
49. Sometimes I'm Rhythm and Sometimes I'm Blues
50. The Dash
51. Those Bus Rides
52. Smile
53. We Are Our Brother's Keeper
54. The Kitchen Table
55. Daddy Was a Good Man
56. I Love You
57. Knowing What I Know Now
58. In the Beginning, God created Just a Man
59. I Often Find My Days Too Short
60. Through Your Eyes
61. What if the World Was Perfect?
62. Life Is What We Make It
63. Fifty Years Later: An Anniversary
64. I Love America
65. Brother to Brother
66. I Wish I Could Have Just One More Day
67. The Power of Prayer
68. Our Children Are Dying

69. Two-Hundred Seventy-Six
70. Words are Powerful
71. Acts of Love?
72. A Moment
73. Identity Crisis
74. God Made You Very Special, and Special You Are
75. Reflection
76. I Am Unapologetically Me
77. What Does Your Tomorrow Look Like?
78. I Love Lincoln University
79. Love Tells a Story
80. I Love Reading
81. Three Shelves
82. A Broken Democracy
83. To God Be the Glory
84. A Mother's Love
85. She Left a Legacy

1

Mama Prayed

Mama knew it would be hard to become a man
Mama knew it would be especially hard to become
a Black man
Mama knew how challenging and difficult it would
be to grow from being a baby into a boy
And a boy into a young man
And from a young man into a man
Mama knew how difficult it would be
to become a good man
Mama knew God had given her a tough assignment
And she knew she couldn't fail
She made a promise to herself to not fail
Mama was committed to her assignment
Mama prayed!
Mama prayed!
Mama prayed!
Mama did what she had to do
To raise her gift from God
Mama promised God she was going to turn this
boy into a strong Black man
Mama was scared
Mama had fears
And Mama had many tears
But even through the tears
Mama prayed!
Mama prayed!
Mama prayed!
Mama vowed to save her gift
from the ills of the world
Mama was not going to allow her gift
To become a statistic or a victim
Daddy was gone
And even when Daddy was there
Daddy was gone

You see, Daddy never grew up himself
Spending his whole life battling his demons
Fighting his own shortcomings
and running the streets
Mama had to pretty much do it alone
But Mama refused to fail
Mama prayed!
Mama prayed!
Mama prayed!
Mama knew what life had in store for her son
She knew the struggles he would face
And the obstacles that could block his path
She knew what the world was offering a Black man
She had to prepare him for what he would face
Mama knew it wouldn't be easy
So she taught him lessons
that would last a life time
Mama nourished
Mama encouraged
Mama protected
Mama supported
Mama taught
But most of all, mama loved
More than anything Mama loved
And it was that love and those numerous prayers
That turned her baby boy into a man
Mama didn't fail
She remained committed to her calling
And because she took her title of mother seriously
And understood who God had designed her to be
That little baby that Mama once held
Became a strong man

2

Mama Was Always There

From my beginning
To her end
Mama was always there
Through the good times and bad
Ups and downs
No matter what
Mama was there
When I was an embryo
She nourished me
When I was a child
She guided and developed me
When I was sick
She cared for me
And when I was hungry
She provided food for me
Mama was always there
She is gone now
But she will never be forgotten
I am who I am
Because
Mama was always there

3

Motivation

Motivation is the action
The energy, the motor, the push
That helps us to reach our full potential
Motivation is that incentive that encourages us all
To be all that we can be
And more than we ever expected to be
Motivation is our fuel
It ignites the starter, it cranks the engine
It propels one's life on a journey of dreams
Motivation is the dream maker, the goal setter
And the mountain climber
Motivation gives us the confidence to succeed
The drive to achieve
The vision to overcome
And the quest to conquer
Being motivated is a nice way of telling one's self
"I love you."
Motivation is the source of the smile in the mirror
After doing what was set out to be done
It is the look of achievement on the face
After doing the impossible
It is the root of the reason in being able to say
"I'm Happy."
With motivation, all things are possible
Motivation isn't saying, "I'm the best."
But it's feeling and knowing
I'm the best that I can be
Motivation is as deep as choosing
Whether to live or exist
Motivation is one of the keys to life
Motivation is the desire to make a positive difference
Motivation is the inspiration to make life truly special

4

I Believe in Love

I believe in love
I believe in the beauty of love
I believe in the depth of love
And I believe in the simplicity of love
I believe in the magic of love
I believe in the power of love
I believe in the realness of love
I believe in love
And its ability to make you do the unexplainable
I believe in the glow of love
And how you can always recognize that look of love
I believe in the excitement of love
I believe in the joy of love
And I believe in the emotions and feelings of love
I understand the hurt that love can bring
But I believe in the restoration of love
And love's ability to repair itself
When one has been damaged by love
I believe in the healing power of love
And how true love can make difficult times right
I believe that love can make every day special
I believe in love and how it penetrates the heart
Enters the sanctuary of the chambers of the heart
And touches the inner thoughts of the mind
I believe in how awesome love is
And how it can make the worst days beautiful
I guess I just believe in love

5

Mama's Words

She always knew what to say
When to say it
And how to say it
And her words were always strong
Strong with love and wisdom
Mama's words were strong
They were always plain and simple
Yet her words were always so deep
Her words were meaningful
And her words had an impact
An impact that helped to mold and develop
Mama's words were always
Caring, challenging, encouraging, motivating
They had a way of making you feel special
Mama's words taught about right and wrong
Mama's words had purpose
Mama knew the importance of sharing her wisdom
She knew her lessons and experiences from life
Could help make the lives for others better
Mama's words showed her love
For all of those she loved
And with whom she crossed paths
Mama's words defined her as a mother
Mama's words defined her as woman
Her words were her way of sharing her faith
Her words were her way of sharing her journey
Her words were her way of expressing her love
Her words were her way of expressing her support
Her words were her way of nurturing
And touching those she loved so much –
Especially family
Mama's words came free of cost
Mama's words were real
Mama's words came from her heart

Mama's words had a way of staying with you
And even when her time was up
She left her words behind
There was nothing like mama's words
Mama's words were those responses you heard
When no one was around
That guided you to do what you needed to do
Or gave you that perfect answer or advice
Just when you needed it
Even though she was no longer around
Her words were always there
And will always be there
Because mama's words were not spoken in vain
Mama's words were strong

6

When Mama Cooked

When mama cooked
She made memories that lasted a lifetime
When mama cooked
People gathered
People socialized
People laughed
People reminisced
When mama cooked
It kept the family close
It healed you when you were sick or hurt
It lifted you up when you were down
People always left her meals feeling encouraged
When mama cooked
She showed her love for family and friends
She recognized when family needed family
And how a good meal brought the family together
Mama knew the power of a good meal
Mama knew the path to the heart
Was through the stomach
Mama knew that satisfying the appetite
Made everything right
When mama cooked
People just came around
Family and friends
Black people and white people
Church folks and sinners
It didn't matter who you were
You didn't even have to know her
If you were around, she told you to fix a plate
Sit down and enjoy it!
Everyone was family when mama cooked
And there was always enough food
Chicken, ham, fried fish, and meatloaf
Pork chops, ribs, chitterlings, and pig feet

Collard greens, cabbage, and black-eyed peas
Fried okra, butter beans, green beans, lima beans
Mashed potatoes and sweet potatoes
And let's not forget the dessert
Apple pie, sweet potato pie, pound cake
And banana pudding
When mama cooked
She made the time special
And she created memories
That would last a lifetime

7
I Am Who I Am

In retrospect
I am who I am
And that is all I can be
Uniquely created
Defined, but undefined
Standing strong and not falling for just anything
Not falling for everything
Never compromising who I am
Or what I believe
I am who I am
Focused on reaching my full potential
Conscious of those
Who have traveled this road before me
So that I can be where I am today
Fully aware that this journey isn't near completion
Knowing that I have a role to play
In this continued journey
I am who I am
Secure in my identity
Focused on fulfilling my dreams
And fully aware of why I must be all I can be
I am who I am
Never giving up on who I am
Mentally prepared to take on all of life's challenges
Learning from my failures and shortcomings
Realizing that I am far from flawless
Realizing that I have made mistakes
And will make more mistakes
I am who I am
Strong enough to admit that I am not perfect
And that I do at times fall below the expectations
That have been set for me
Revealing my weaknesses
But even in my lows there are still highs
I am who I am

Not backing away from the fact
That I am a role model
And that I do have an obligation
To pave the road for those young people
Who are coming behind me
Understanding it takes an entire community
To raise a child
Understanding that I am a part of my community
Understanding that I can never forget my journey
And that I can never forget where I've come from
I am who I am
Taking a stand for what is right
Being a voice
Fighting against the wrongs of this world
Realizing that if I'm not a part of the solution
Then I'm a part of the problem
I am who I am
A man striving to be who God designed me to be
A man who desires to be a light in this dark world
A man who is trying hard to do his best
In all of the roles that he has accepted
So in retrospect
I am who I am
And that is all I can be
Uniquely created
Defined, but undefined
Standing strong and not falling for just anything
Not falling for everything
Never compromising who I am
Or what I believe
I am who I am

8

You Live and You Learn

A moment of reflection
About life and what life has become
Will bring everyone to the realization
That life is what we make of it
Life is what life is
We spend years
Planning and dreaming
Of what we hope our lives will one day become
But sometimes, at the crossroads of life
We suffer from broken dreams and plans
And after those broken dreams and plans
Life doesn't always turn out
The way we thought it would
Sometimes life takes us down roads
We never thought we would have to travel
And experiences that we never thought
Would knock on our door
And sometimes life throws a curve
We never thought life
Could cause hurt and pain
We never thought life
Could be so disruptive
We never thought life
Could be so brutal in teaching and giving lessons
We never thought life could be so hard
And not become the fulfilled dreams or plans
We always thought would become our reality
We never thought
Because of choices and decisions
Life could take turns and U-turns
That could change the direction of our plans
And affect the rest of our lives
We sometimes approach life like it is a game
And in the beginning
We enjoy the newness of the game

We enjoy the spontaneity, excitement
Fun and good times the game has to offer
But the newness of the game sometimes wears off
And we have to deal with the fact and realization
That the game was a bad choice and a bad decision
An error and a mistake
That will impact what we thought life would be
But you see
Life is what we make of it
Life is what life is
Choices and decisions
Planning and dreaming
Sometimes fulfilled
Sometimes broken
But when it is all said and done
You live and you learn

9

Can We Call it the Blues?

Is it a contradiction to call blue my favorite color
Yet sometimes have the audacity to say
"I have the blues"?
Being a lover of the many shades of blue
From the royal blue of my fraternity
To the midnight blue of that BMW
To the sky blue of the North Carolina Tar Heels
I must admit I have a love for blue
No matter what shade
There is just something about that blue
But why is it called the blues
When things aren't right?
It's always the blues when life is down and not up
When the beginning of the week opens the door
To drama and frustration
Why is it the blues
When a beautiful day's sunshine
Is stolen by the day's rain?
Why is it the blues
When we expect the best and the best never comes
Or when we expect the best
And the worse shows up?
I guess we call it the blues when the person
Who is supposed to be your rib
Acts more like a pain in the butt
Most people would definitely say
You have some form of the blues
Is it the blues or can we call it the blues
When the job that is a blessing
Feels more like a prison sentence?
It's not an issue of not being thankful for the job
But sometimes people have a way of turning a
Good day into a nightmare
And that is when it starts to resemble the blues

When you're tired of people not doing right
When you're tired of the same nonsense everyday
From the games people play
To what we see on television everyday
The blues!
But the funny thing about the blues
Is that most of us don't know
We do not have the right to say we have the blues!
I've never heard of a dying person
Who has been given six months to live
Say, "I have the blues."
I've never heard of those survivors of genocide
In the many persecuted parts of Africa
Talk of having the blues
And I've never heard the screams of having the
Blues coming out of the walls of the many prisons
In this country that freezes time
For so many of our brothers and sisters
But as Brother Gil Scott Heron would say
"It's a Blues Year!"
So I say, let's stop abusing my favorite color
When you're having a really bad day
And you feel like escaping from reality
Let's not say we have the blues
When the week starts off
Like you're in the middle of the eye of a storm
And you're being hit by a hurricane
Let's not say we have the blues
When there is no money coming in
And a payday won't be arriving anytime soon
Let's not call it the blues
When you feel like you want to holler
And throw up both of your hands
Let's not look for a member of the blues family
To identify that current state of frustration
So instead of calling every low point
In our lives the blues
Let's just say, "Thank you, Lord!"
And realize that regardless of how bad things are
We are still blessed

**And if being blessed
Could be identified as the blues
Then I guess it is not a contradiction
To call blue my favorite color**

10

Young, Gifted, and Black

Young, gifted, and Black
When will you realize?
When will you understand?
That just because you have money and fame
Doesn't give you the right to act insane?
Just because you can play a game
Or can kick some words over a beat
Does that mean you are now above the law?
Just because you are a media star
Are you no longer accountable for negative actions
Nor responsible for unruly behaviors?
Just because you are young, gifted, and Black
Doesn't mean you don't know how to act
Your future is bright
Your potential is unlimited
But to jeopardize your future
And for what?
Street creditability?
Wake up! Young, gifted, and Black
Because God has given you a gift
And as easily as your fortunate situation has come
It can just as easily go
You have been given an opportunity to shine
But you would rather shine in negativity
In disgrace and shame
Rather than portray respect
And a positive self-image
So hold your head up, pull your pants up
And have some pride and self-respect
Realize that you are an example
To those who idolize you
Young, gifted, and Black
Realize that you have a responsibility
And much is expected of you

So straighten up and step up
And be all that you can be
And what you can be is something positive
And something special
Reach your full potential
And show the world what it *should* mean to be
Young, gifted, and Black

God Gave Us Mothers

God loves us so much, He gave us mothers
God knew when He brought us into this world
We all would need a special kind of love
God knew that who He created in His own image
Would need a lot of care and nurturing
To be whom He designed them to be
Every woman that has ever had a child
God has given the ability to love in a way
That is different from any other love
God has given every mother the ability to love
Unconditionally
God has blessed mothers with the ability to love
With an amazing love
God has put something in the heart of mothers
That will make them both cry and smile
While welcoming their new child into the world
God has blessed mothers with the ability
To carry a child for nine months
And love that child for a lifetime
God gave mothers the ability to feed their child
Right out of the womb
God gave mothers the ability to educate
And prepare their child for the life they will face
God gave mothers the ability to offer life lessons
Even when they take a while to be received
God gave mothers the ability to chase fears away
During sleepless nights
God gave mothers the strength to lift up their child
When they have fallen down
God gave mothers the right words
When advice and encouragement are needed
For God so loved the world
That He gave us mothers
Mothers who would accept their assignment

And their role to be the best mothers
God gave us mothers to guide, protect, teach
God gave us mothers to love
As only a good mother can
God knew exactly what we would need
So He gave us all a mother to fulfill that need
God knew we all needed a mother
Like we would need food and water to survive
God knew the world would provide many
Challenging moments and difficult times
So He gave us mothers
Mothers that were instilled with the inner strength
To provide us with what we needed
Mothers that would be there
Just when we needed them
God also knew that all mothers
Were not going to be who He designed them to be
So He put in the heart of all women
The ability to be a mother to a child
That is not her own
God knew that every mother
Would not be a good mother
Yet He knew that every child needed
The love of a mother
So He blessed many hurt, lonely
And neglected children
With women whom they could call *mother*
And whom they could call their own
God loves us so much that He gave us something
That came from His heart
And touched our hearts
God loves us so much
He gave us a gift from heaven
God loves us so much that He gave us mothers

Hip Hop

Is Hip Hop the problem
Or are we as a society the problem?
Have we failed to ensure
That Hip Hop wouldn't succumb
To the ills of our society?
Society has failed in its responsibility
To safeguard and protect Hip Hop
What can exist can only exist if allowed to exist
So society must be held accountable
For what Hip Hop has become
The culture of Hip Hop isn't all negative
But it has evolved into something
That is strongly influenced by negativity
Society has allowed Hip Hop to be transformed
Hip Hop was not rooted or meant to be something
Infested by negativity
Hip Hop wasn't birthed glorifying crime
Violence and a gangster lifestyle
Hip Hop wasn't about degrading women
Explicit sex and foul language
Hip Hop used to be about something
Hip Hop started out as something truly artistic
Something truly creative
Hip Hop was rap
Rhythm and poetry
Hip Hop was art
Totally unique and beautiful
Hip Hop was dance
Energetic and alive
Hip Hop was a message
Always positive, fun, or deep
Hip Hop started out as a real positive movement
Something that brought people together
But society has allowed it to poison our people

Society has allowed Hip Hop
To become an instrument of self-destruction
Society has allowed BET (Black Exploitation Television)
And MTV (Manipulation Television)
To dictate how Hip Hop would be defined
Society has allowed companies and advertisers
That are making millions off of Hip Hop
To exploit Hip Hop
And control the image of Hip Hop
Society needs a stronger influence on the media
A stronger influence on the advertisers
And companies that are controlling Hip Hop
Society needs a stronger influence
On the Hip Hop artists
Society needs to set a standard
That cannot be compromised
Society needs to be responsible
And who is society?
Everyone that has a love for people
Everyone that has a love for Hip Hop
Society must save Hip Hop
So that it can be all it was meant to be
Something beautiful
Something creative
Something unique
Something with a positive effect on our society

13

No Child Left Behind

If we are to have no child left behind
We have to remember
How it once took a community
To raise and prepare a child for life
We have to make a commitment
To be involved in the lives of our children
We have to be that positive primary influence
We have to be that positive example
We have to be that positive role model
We have to let them know we care about them
And that we are going to be a part of their lives
We cannot afford to lose another young person
To the ills of our world
We cannot afford to lose another young person
To violence, prison, or AIDS
We cannot afford to have another young person
Drop out of school or become pregnant
We cannot afford to allow a bleak picture
To become bleaker
We have to make a commitment
To save future generations
We cannot depend on our government
To save our children and young people
We have to save our own
We have to mentor our own
We have to develop and train our own
We have to teach our own to learn
And not just prepare them for a test
We have to be involved in their education
And make sure they are being taught
Not just being passed through the school system
We have to fight for their rights
And provide them with what they need to succeed
We have to screen them from the poison

That is broadcasted through our media
We have to protect them from the negativity
That is spread through movies, music, and videos
We have to protect our children and young people
From a society that would rather exploit them
And make money off of them
Than to help them reach their full potential
We have to step up
Because we all have a responsibility
And we all are role models
Because
We must have no child left behind

14

Katrina

Hurricane Katrina was an act of God
But the condition and state of New Orleans
Was an act of neglect
The city of New Orleans failed
The state of Louisiana failed
The federal government and FEMA failed
America failed
Years have passed
And New Orleans is still not the city it used to be
Anniversary after anniversary
Reminds us of what we would rather forget
The eye of this devastating storm named Katrina
Remains fixed over the city of New Orleans
And the nightmare continues
For those that called the Big Easy home
Many people from New Orleans
Are still scattered across America
Displaced and misplaced
Unable to return to what was once their home
And in the midst of their despair
They were called refugees - and treated as such
Because in reality, the "State of Emergency"
For New Orleans was a joke
There continues to be a slow response
For the victims of this great catastrophe
The burden and the level of responsibility
Has been a national disgrace
America has sent millions of dollars
To emergency victims around the world
Yet America has forgotten its own
As the Big Easy struggles to rebuild
St. Bernard Parish and other parts
Of the Lower Ninth Ward
Look worse than war-torn Afghanistan, Iraq

And Syria
The neglect of this great city is overtly shameful
As our government refuses to address
The lack of support for the victims
Of this nightmare called Katrina
The city of New Orleans
And many of its peoples' futures remain uncertain
A city that is known for its beauty and culture
And was the heart and soul of Louisiana
Is now a victim of federal bureaucracy
And blatant neglect
Katrina was a Category 5 hurricane
But because of a slow motion response
And a failure to fully rebuild New Orleans
The aftermath of Katrina
Has also been like a Category 5 hurricane
As New Orleans continues to feels the pain and
Frustration caused by Katrina
The deadliest natural disaster in American history
America must admit that it has
And continues to fail the people of New Orleans
The Big Easy still suffers
Like it has been hit by a hurricane
A hurricane that should be named "Neglect"

15

The Masks

What you see is not always what it may be
The smiles, laughs, and words frequently shared
The masks that so often conceal one's true identity
The masks have become the everyday disguise
At this masquerade ball called life
The masks hide reality with a façade
Often allowing a performance to be so perfect
That it sometimes even fools the performer
The masks will do what they need to do
Whenever they need to do it
In order to keep people fooled
The masks do what they do best
Hiding what is behind the masks
And protecting secrets
The masks allow people
To become fictional characters
Playing whatever role will protect the true identity
Behind the masks
The masks are the symbols of a divided soul
Trying to manage the joys and pains of one's life
The masks hide the blank stares
And enigmatic expressions
Caused by the internal conflict
That is warring against the external silence
The masks consistently perform flawlessly
Whether the performance is scripted
Or unscripted
Whether the performance is planned
Or spontaneous
The masks do what they need to do
And what the audience sees
Is like a reflection in the water
It doesn't see the camouflage

The masks have been used as emotion protectors
And heart protectors
The masks have become a necessary safeguard
For one not being recognized by the audience
For one that nobody knows about
For one who is broken and damaged
For one who is hurting and in pain
For one that nobody sees crying
When there is no one around
The masks hide reality's true existence
From whoever the audience may be
The masks are everything you can't see
The masks are examples of strength and weakness
The masks provide the confidence, dedication
And determination to make it through the day
But are the masks really who people may be?
Sadly, the answer is no!
The masks are worlds apart from the people
Who are behind the masks
The masks have played this role for so long
That they can no longer really relate
To who is really behind the masks
The masks help resist the temptation
To be the people who are behind the masks
And the people behind the masks
Are afraid to take the masks off
But it is time to stop wearing the masks
The people behind the masks must stop
Compromising who they truly are
The people behind the masks
Must deal with the past, confront the present
And accept the challenges of the future
The people behind the masks
Must make the masks
That were worn on a daily basis, faces of the past
So that from this day forward, the faces you see
Will reveal who people truly are
And there will be no more need to wear masks

16

Grandma's Hands

She was a pillar of consistency
What you saw is what you got
Full of love
Always caring
Strong as iron
Feisty as they came
Took nothing from anyone
Life made her tough
She had all of the answers
And knew everything that needed to be known
Despite having just a meager education
Grandma was strong
Grandma grew up when it was hard
Hard life
Hard work
Hard times
But it didn't weaken Grandma
It helped make Grandma stronger
It helped paint the picture of who Grandma was
Because Grandma knew who she was
All that she knew
Was all that she was and it was that simple
God
Family
And her love and support for her family and others
That was Grandma
The backbone of the family
And even in her old age
She was still the strength of the family
Touching children
Grandchildren
And great-grandchildren
Grandma touched many lives
She was the positive motivating force

In everyone's life
She knew what everyone needed
And gave it to them just when it was needed
She knew when to give a word
She knew when to give her opinion
She knew when to give a hug
And she knew when to pray
And if it wasn't for her constant prayers
And open line to God
I don't know where I would be!
Grandma believed in prayer
And she was always praying
She didn't always know exactly what was going on
But somehow she always knew what to pray for
Grandma was always serving
Taking care of home
Raising children
Including those who were not her own
Grandma was always helping others
There were never any strangers in her life
If there was a need to be met she addressed it
Whether she knew you or not
Meeting the needs of others
Was just a part of her life
Grandma was always serving God
Because she believed when you serve others
You were also serving God
And Grandma knew God
It was Grandma's hands
That helped to raise generations
Her hands that were wrinkled by old age
Told her story
Her hands told of a life dedicated to others
They told of her unconditional love
And of her journey
And though Grandma's words were very powerful
Her hands said it all
When you held those old wrinkled hands
You discovered the love from her heart
That could only come from Grandma's hands

17

Beautiful Lady

You are a beautiful lady and so beautiful you are
You are so beautiful
Because your beauty not only reveals who you are
But it reveals whose you are
Your beauty defines you
Your beauty describes you
But most of all, your beauty says, "I belong to God"
Of all of the wonders God has made
There is none that is more beautiful than you
God's light shines through you
Revealing your commitment to glorify Him
In everything you do
The smile He has painted upon your face
Is your symbol to the world
Of your love for God, family, and friends
There is nothing more beautiful than you
Beautiful Lady
Because beauty described is beauty defined
And when you combine the word beautiful
With the word lady
What we have is the definition of you
Your qualities reveal every aspect
Of your inner and outer beauty
The characteristics of your beauty
Highlight all that you are
The intimate relationship
Between the inside and outside of you
Makes you the complete and beautiful lady
That you are
Your beauty is like a poem that touches the heart
Your beauty is like a meaningful song
That chants all of the right things
Your beauty
Is not your stunning physical attributes

Your beauty is not the clothes you wear
Your beauty is not how you arrange your hair
Your beauty is not the depth of your mind
Your beauty is not your high intellect
Your beauty is not your great personality
Your beauty is not your beautiful sense of humor
Your beauty is how you try daily
To live up to God's design for you
You are a beautiful lady and so beautiful you are
God created you to be very special
And very special you have grown to be
Your beauty exceeds
The imagination of my thoughts
Beautiful is in the way you laugh
Beautiful is in the glow in your eyes
Beautiful is your love for the Lord
Beautiful is your strong faith in the Lord
Beautiful are acts of love
That come from your heart
Beautiful are the acts of kindness
That so often remain unseen
Beautiful is your unconditional love
For your family
Beautiful is your dedicated commitment
To your friends
Beautiful is the passion for life
That always glows from you
You are a Beautiful Lady
And this is reflected in all that you do
Your beauty touches hearts
Your beauty influences lives
Your beauty inspires
Your beauty motivates
Your beauty radiates
Your beauty is powerful
Your beauty is limitless
Your beauty is pure
Your beauty is why I love and adore you
You are a beautiful lady
And so beautiful you are

18

Darfur

The world has a crisis
Yet the world doesn't seem to care
In Darfur people are dying and living in fear
Millions of people are living in a desert
And being chased from their homes
The world leaders are aware
But they leave this issue alone
How many people have to die
Before the world reacts and responds?
This just doesn't make sense
Does the world have a double standard
When it comes to Africa?
We rushed into Bosnia, Kosovo and Iraq
But not into Africa!
For some reason we just won't go
Two million people dying in Rwanda
And we won't go
The same in Somalia and Sudan
And we still won't go
Millions are still dying in Africa
But for some reason Africa is ignored
The world, and even our President
Acknowledge the problems
Even calling it genocide
But is this just a word?
The world sits back and does nothing about this
International crime
Obviously people dying is not enough
To make the world care
It must depend on where the people are from
And whether there are any economic benefits
Or natural resources that can be exploited
Before America will respond
Only thousands dead in Bosnia and Kosovo
Yet America responded

Like Iraq, we justified our response
Must we say more!
Troops, sanctions, and resources were sent
Because they said it was genocide
Or the governments were corrupt
It was all on the news
The USA Today and other media sources
Reported daily of their horrors
But with Darfur and other African nations
There are hardly any actions
We hear and see very little on the news
Concerning the African crisis
Millions of people are dying in Rwanda
Sudan and Somalia
Yet ABC, CBS, NBC, Fox
And CNN broadcast little
In between the latest drama in American news
And in between the Oscars and the weather
A report shows that Darfur is in crisis
But the world doesn't seem to care about the crisis
Few troops, few sanctions, and very little money
Are budgeted to address these crises in Africa
So the facts remain
People are suffering in Africa
And especially Darfur
And sadly the world doesn't seem to care

19

A Generation Lost

Dark clouds hide the sunshine
Of many bright futures
Many young people live lives
As endangered species
Their futures look so very bleak
Bad choices and poor decisions made now
Dictate what forever will be
Not realizing how the past, present, and future
Connect to one another
Not realizing how embracing a negative culture
Can welcome a lifetime of unforeseen despair
Not realizing the challenges faced in this world
Very seldom forgive and forget
A generation lost
Our past weeps and we, the present
Sit back and watch many of those
Who should be our future
Go from the cradle to the grave
Watching as generation after generation
Is falling victim to the self-destruction
And self-hatred that is stealing so many futures
How do we change this reality?
We sit in our inconsistent state of concern
Living our lives with the attitude and mindset
That "We Have Overcome"
Unconsciously unaware
That we're losing those we love
That we're losing our young gifted minds
That we're losing our future
A generation lost
We must apologize
To our young brothers and sisters
We must apologize for allowing them to be at-risk
We must apologize

For the high number of drop-outs
We must apologize
For allowing so many of them to be unemployable
We must apologize
For the addictions they struggle with day after day
We must apologize
For the criminal records that will plague them
We must apologize
For allowing a mental health system
To label so many of our young people
With mental health diagnoses
Young people
We owe you an apology
For not protecting your future
A generation lost
But the blame is not all ours
You young people must also accept responsibility
With your dresses up high and pants hanging low
With your "I don't care attitude"
Revealing to the world
That "I have no respect for anyone or anything"
You don't even realize the crisis you're in
The self-inflicted state of mental incarceration
Or the underachievement and unfulfilled potential
That is stealing the fulfillment of dreams
And bright futures
A generation lost
Wake up my young brothers and sisters!
Self-defeating and self-destructive behaviors
Should not define who you are
Embrace the gifts God has given you
Take the right path
Find your way
You don't have to be a statistic
And your future doesn't have to be bleak
You can change the perception of who you are
You can change the societal disparities
And socioeconomic realities
By being the best you can be
Change your reality

And you can make your future what it should be
You can be someone very special
You were not born to fail
You have a better story than one with a sad ending
So let us all wake up
And make a commitment for change
A commitment for better days
And of lives full of success
By working together, the future should be bright
And the story should have a better title than
"A Generation Lost"

Slow Reaction, No Reaction!

Slow reaction, no reaction
The world is guilty of neglect once again
This time it is Nigeria
Two hundred seventy-six young girls
Kidnapped from school
Weeks passed
As their parents prayed continuously
For their safe return
Nigeria is ignored and neglected
It was almost like what is going on in Nigeria
Is not even happening
But the crisis in Nigeria is very real
And we should respond
We must remember what happened in Rwanda
And how no response
Cost a million people their lives
We must remember what is happening in Darfur
And the fact that people are still dying there
There are too many atrocities occurring in Africa
To have an international response that is delayed
People are dying and being displaced
Corrupt dictators and governments
Are abusing their power and control
Religious persecution, ethnic cleansing
And famine are stealing lives
And the devastation caused by HIV and AIDS
Is not getting the attention it deserves
The past and the present
Tell painful stories of Africa
Stories of Angola, Darfur, Ghana, Kenya
South Africa, Zaire, Nigeria, Ethiopia, Sudan
Uganda, Liberia, Botswana, Rwanda, Zimbabwe,
Somalia and Sierra Leone
And then we are faced with another crisis

This time it is Nigeria
But is not responding
As the families of two hundred seventy-six girls
Cried for their freedom?
Is there a slow reaction
Or is there no reaction?
If history and the media are accurate
Then the past and the present tell us
And we must ask, "Does Africa matter?"
How many people must die?
How many children must die?
How many people must go hungry?
The media and the press reported
On genocide and famine
But the world acts like it doesn't care
And we continue to have
Slow reaction, no reaction

21

God Gave Me a Gift

God gave me a gift
And that gift became a part of me
God gave me someone special
And now my eyes see
How God gave me this gift
So that I could become me
God gave me someone special
That loved me unconditionally
Her love was deep
And it came from her heart
A deep devotion that I knew from the start
She loved me truly
And it came from within
She was the definition of love
And her love had no end
God gave me this gift
And it became so much to me
This gift became my teacher
My counselor
And my friend
Full of wisdom that enriched my life
The example she set will be with me my whole life
My gift made me feel like I could do anything
My gift made me feel I could be all I could be
She gave me strength and security
We had a bond and she protected me
She was the blessing that God had sent for me
The gift had sacrificed and endured for me
She did what she had to do
So I could be all I could be
As I think about the gift that God had given me
I won't cry, but instead I will smile
Because God planned this gift just for me
A gift from God

Personally designed for and given to me
A gift that I know will always be with me
Even though my gift is gone
My gift will never be far
Because God gave me a gift
And that gift became a part of me

There is a Pulse in Haiti

Through the sounds of crying from the Haitians
Whose land has been stained by the blood
Of one of this world's greatest tragedies
There is a pulse
Through the sounds of screams
Amidst people finding out their loved ones
Are gone forever
There is a pulse
Through the sounds of children
Calling for their parents
And parents calling for their children
Fearing their calls may not get a response
There is a pulse
In the toughest of times
Behind the tears that could fill a lake
And through the echoes of crying
In the darkness of despair
There is a pulse that is strong
Fueled by the blood pumping
Into the heart of a nation
Haiti's heart beats strongly
Haiti!
The example of freedom and liberty
The world refuses to acknowledge
And though abused and not respected
For their contributions to the world
Haiti and its people remain a symbol of courage
And a symbol of strength
During defining moments and great adversity
Haiti has shown it is strong and not irrelevant
Haiti has a heart that beats like a drum
Through the sounds of so much pain and suffering
You will hear the sounds of the voices of Haiti
Proclaiming that an earthquake

Wasn't strong enough to destroy their nation
Because Haitians know how to survive
Though the journey may be long
And their road may be rough
There will be a tomorrow for Haiti
Because Haiti and the people of Haiti are strong
And there is a pulse
Haiti is strengthened by its history
Because when Haiti looks back
It helps them to move forward
Haiti has seen two hundred years of poverty
And two hundred years of oppression
Haiti has been betrayed and neglected
Haiti has seen devastating hurricanes and storms
Yet Haiti has rebuilt and reconstructed
When you look at Haiti's past and present
Its then and its now
You will discover Haiti's lost and found
And as history speaks the truth
It will tell the story of the plight of a nation
Whose heart has beat strongly since its birth
Though there have been many times
That seemed like Haiti's worst
Haiti's pulse is still there
Despite so much death and destruction
The spirit of Haiti has survived and is alive
Because the people of Haiti are no ordinary people
The people of Haiti are strong
And there is a pulse in Haiti

23

Haiti: The Forgotten Symbol of Freedom and Strength

"Where there is unity there is strength"
And for a nation with a history
A little over 200 years old
Haiti's motto says it all
Haiti has had its share of trials
But Haiti has been strong and has persevered
Echoes of the past paint a vivid picture
Of the troubled history of this nation
Haiti knows suffering well
Haiti's tears have fallen often
But history tells the story of a nation of people
Who have been courageous, strong, and unified
A nation of people that understands how to survive
Haiti: The forgotten symbol
Of freedom and strength
The nation that fought for its freedom
From slavery to freedom to the birth of a nation
The world's first Black republic
And independent nation
But a nation that has always suffered
From Toussaint L'Ouverture
The patriot and liberator of Haiti
To one of the poorest nations in the world
From resisting slavery, colonialism
Foreign exploitation and intervention
To Papa Doc, Baby Doc, and Aristide
From the political instability of corrupt leaders
To being the victim of political oppression
Failed governments and national debts
From being a Caribbean beauty
To being a haven for natural disasters
Though this impoverished nation has suffered
Haiti has remained the symbol of strength

"Where there is unity there is strength"
Even when Haiti became a picture
Of death and devastation
And the images caused by a category 7 earthquake
Were unimaginable and difficult to comprehend
The people of Haiti came together
And remained courageous and strong
With their capital Port-Au-Prince destroyed
And the collapsed presidential palace
Symbolizing a wounded nation
The people of Haiti, in their weakness
Have remained a picture of strength
This nation was limited in its capacity to help itself
Yet the plight of Haiti caused the world to respond
Because as the Haitians cried
The world cried with them
And as all Haitians know
"Where there is unity there is strength"
Because out of the darkness of the night
Comes the light of the morning sun
And the rainbow after a storm
So stay strong Haiti, and remember your history
Because you are a nation of people
That has always been strong
Haiti will survive, because
"Where there is unity there is strength"

24

Missing

A father should be a noun and a verb
A father should embrace the title of father
And practice what the title calls him to be
A father understands the responsibility
And significance of being a father
A father accepts all that comes with being a father
A father accepts the good with the bad
And the joys with the pains
A father is a caretaker, protector
Provider and teacher
A father is chosen and is given a gift from God
But sadly, there are many men
Who have chosen to not accept the gift
There are too many fathers
Who are only biological fathers
They are not fathers because of their efforts
They are fathers because they planted their seed
There are too many fathers
Who have made a choice
A choice not to love, build foundations
Or make memories with their children
Fathers who have chosen to be invisible men
In the lives of their children
Fathers who are missing in action
Fathers who are missing
From the lives of their children
Fathers who have failed to comprehend
That fatherhood begins at conception
And will last for the rest of their lives
Fathers whose children will be left
With a broken legacy to follow
And with many unfulfilled dreams
Fathers who continue to contribute to an epidemic
That is damaging and destroying the lives

Of so many children
Fathers who have taken the "happy"
Out of Happy Father's Day
Too many fathers are missing
The father is supposed to be the dream keeper
But what happens
When the one who should be the dream keeper
Disappears or fails to accept the assignment?
Fathers fail to realize that in their absence
A child is missing something very special
So many men are misaligned
With God's design of what a father should be
So many mothers do their best to play the dual role
Of a mother and a father
So many children living their lives
Without a loving, responsible, and active father
Far too many children
Only dream of having a father in their lives
A good father can help develop a son
And steer a son in a positive direction
A good father can reveal to a daughter
What a real man looks like
And show her how a queen is to be treated
A good father assures the mother of his children
That fatherlessness will never be associated
With his fatherhood
Too many fathers are failing to fulfill the intimacy
That should exist between a father and his seed
Fathers must understand that it is important
To be a part of their children's lives
Fathers must make a commitment
To not just be a father
But to be the best father they can be
Fathers must stop making excuses
For why they cannot be a good father
Fathers must develop a parenting relationship
With the mother of his children
Fathers must understand the importance
Of being connected with their children
Fathers must feel the pain caused

**By being an absent father
Too many fathers are child-support fathers
And nothing more
Too many fathers are putting themselves
Before their children
Too many fathers have no idea
Of what it takes to be a father
But it is time to learn
Too many fathers know little to nothing
About their kids
And too many children know little to nothing
About their fathers
All because too many fathers have gone missing**

25

Mama Loved to Hug

Mama loved hugging almost as much as her family
It didn't matter if she was greeting you
Or saying goodbye
It always started and ended with a hug
Mama believed in hugs
Hugs helped to define who she was to everyone
Mama loved to hug
And it didn't matter who you were
If you stood in front of her long enough
You would receive a hug
Mama believed her hugs were meant for everyone
It didn't matter where you were from
It didn't matter what color you were
Her hugs united the hearts of people
Her hugs warmed the hearts of those
Who crossed her path
Whether she knew you or not
You were going to be hugged
Her hugs were special
And you never forgot them
They were as memorable
As meeting someone famous
Or going somewhere for the first time
At the mention of Mama's name
The first thing that came to mind
Was her unforgettable hugs
Hugs that would often squeeze you
With an expression of her love
Mama loved to hug
Mama would just open her arms
And wrap them around you
Giving you some of her love
Next to praising and worshiping God
Hugging was Mama's favorite action to express

Mama used hugging as a way of putting smiles
On the faces of people
Mama used hugging as a way of lifting up people
Who were feeling down
Mama used hugging to encourage people
And letting them know it would be all right
Mama used hugging as a way of saying I love you
Because Mama loved everyone
Her hugging was for everyone
Her hugging was a symbol of her love
And those hugs became a piece of her legacy
Mama's embracing others made memories
And they changed lives
The hugs were Mama's way of inviting you
Into her life
A life full of a contagious love that infected you
And had an impact on your life
Mama's hugs were real
And they made the most beautiful memories
Mama's hugs were given to not be forgotten
Mama's hugs were happiness in an ugly world
Mama's hugs were a little joy for everyone
Whose lives she touched
Mama's hugs were so special
They remained long after she took her last breath
Mama's hugs are a little bit of her spirit
That she left behind for us to remember
How we are to love each other
Her hugs had the ability to intimately share
What it usually took words to say
Mama loved to hug
And those hugs were her way of saying,
"I love and care about you."
I am so thankful that Mama loved to hug

26

Life Goes On

Sometimes you think you know people
But in reality, you don't know them at all
Sometimes you give so much of yourself
But in reality, all you do is give too much
And time shows they really don't care at all
Sometimes you become emotionally connected
And all it does is cause hurt and pain
Sometimes you trust people
And you later realize
You shouldn't have trusted at all
Sometimes you give your love
Your thoughts
Your feelings
And emotions
And when it's all said and done
And you take the time to examine and reflect
On the course your life has just traveled
You realize so much time has been wasted
It has been said that people will be people
So don't be surprised by what people will say or do
People will attempt to try you and use you
People will hurt you
People will even tell you they love you
The games people play!
I don't know what tomorrow will bring
It may be joy
It may be pain
It may be a beautiful day
It may be rain
I don't know what tomorrow will bring
But whatever tomorrow brings
Make it the best tomorrow it can be
Do not allow those who have brought hurt
Into your life to defeat you
You are strong and you are a survivor

Keep smiling and standing tall
You thought the people were real
But don't allow the experiences to steal your joy
And although you now realize
They were just performing
Just thank God for carrying you through
Because life goes on

My Words Are Me

My words are a personal and poetic journey
Reflecting my past, present, and future
My words reflect my emotional thoughts
My words reflect my spiritual thoughts
My words are the expression of my joys and pains
My words are the realities of my highs and lows
My words are my hopes and pieces of my dreams
My words are my fears
My words are the melancholy
That sometimes appears
My words are a symbol of my commitment
To reach my full potential
My words are my search for sunshine
On a cloudy day
My words are the heartbeats that define who I am
My words are my inspiration
To lift my voice and sing
My words are my way of truly being free
My words are the influences of the past
That guide me towards my future
My words are a light
For my African American journey
My words are the memories of my loved ones
My words are the reminders
Of the shackled chains of a painful past
My words honor the many people
Who paved the way for a better future
My words are what I stand for
My words are what I refuse to compromise
My words are my knowledge
Of yesterday, today, and tomorrow
My words are a description of the total me
My words are my discernment
Of right versus wrong

My words are my creative mind
My innovative mind
And my spiritual mind
My words are my trips down memory lane
My words are my lifetime of experiences
Whether good or bad
My words are about matters
And intimacies of the heart
My words are often about love
My words are about the internal feelings
That only being in love could bring
My words are about my communications
Of one heart to another heart
My words are descriptions
Of my thoughts and feelings on love
My words are reminiscent of the depth of love
My words are the many lessons
I have learned in life
My words are the strength to hold my head up high
My words are what connect the dots
In helping me to understand this world
My words are my faith and trust in God
My words are my understanding
That through God, anything is possible
My words are my celebrations
My words are my sorrows
My words are my way of saying
"This too shall pass."
My words are my way of saying
"Everything will be all right"
My words are an open book of me
My words are real
My words are true
My words are my legacy
My words are who I am
My words are me

28

A Father

It really does not bother me
When the F-word is used to describe me
I know who I am and I know what I am
I know I am not perfect
And I know I make mistakes
But I am who I am
And I am not ashamed of who I am
So if you want to use the F-word to describe me
I can accept it and I can handle it
If you want to call me the F-word
Then I will welcome the title
In a society where titles are thrown around loosely
I refuse to be an example
Of what many people want the world to believe
And I will not be included
In any negative stereotypes
With my hands clenched and my eyes closed
I pray to God for the strength
To not be less than I should be
I know I am called to be responsible
I know I am called to be an example
I know I am just the vessel that carries the lessons
That help build a strong foundation
So I pray I am consistently consistent
In being faithful to who I am supposed to be
I pray that I will be the light that brightens a life
And protects a soul
May I be a dream keeper who instills
The beautiful sound of music
Coming from the heart
May I be the guide who leads
From one destination to the next
On this journey of life
May I always be consciously aware

Of what is required of me for this assignment
May I always take the assignment seriously
And may the journey's assignment strengthen me
So if you want to use the F-word to describe me
I don't mind
Personally, I have grown fond of it
I am often inspired when I hear it
And just thinking about it
I'm motivated to give my best effort
Many people cannot handle hearing the F-word
Because so many people have failed
To be who they were supposed to be
Many people do not have a desire
To be more than a neglectful world donor
Many people have not accepted the many positives
That come with being called the F-word
Due to past hurts, many people have continued
A cycle of hurt and neglect
But for me, the F-word is proudly embraced
I thank God every day for each time
I am associated with the F-word
Being chosen was a gift
And this gift has helped to make me who I am
I will always honor my gift
By being the best that I can be
I will always sacrifice myself because of my gift
But most of all, I will show love because of my gift
I will love with all of the love I have to give
Because being called the F-word
Does not bother me
Father!
And I take this title seriously
I enjoy being a father
I love being a father
And I am proud to be a father
A parent, provider, protector, and teacher
An advisor, confidant, and the king of four hearts
Having the wisdom to offer direction
And having the wisdom to offer understanding
Being a father has taught me the importance

Of being a good father
It has helped me to realize
That I cannot fail in this role
It is that realization that strengthens me
To be the best father I can be
Every biological father is not a father
All men are not deserving of the title of father
It is a title that is earned
But all men have not earned the respect
Or the right to be called father
So I must say, it feels really good
When I hear the F-word used regarding me
Father!
Yes! I am proud to be a father
And Yes! I am a proud father

29

Racial Profiling:
A Reality for Many

We hold these truths to be self-evident
That all men are created equally
But sadly, our Declaration of Independence didn't
Declare that all people would be treated equally
In America there is an ugly reality
And that reality is that race is a factor
And racial profiling does exist
Being targeted and routinely stopped or followed
Just because of skin color
Just because of being Black
This reality that has become a terrible experience
For so many in America
Just because a person's skin is of a darker hue
Among God's rainbow of complexions
Increases the chances
Of being social injustice victims
Almost one hundred fifty years after slavery ended
Almost fifty years since the March on Washington
More than forty years since the death of King
And since a Civil Rights revolution
Even as our first Black President perseveres
During his two terms in office
Maybe it's America that needs a teachable moment
Race still matters in our society
Racism still haunts America
And racial profiling is as strong as ever
Daily acts of racial harassment remind us
Of the racial injustices of the past
And that a great racial divide still exists today
Being followed, stopped, questioned, searched
And even arrested
Solely on the basis of color and race
Often with no probable cause and without reason

Is a way of life for many in America!
Acts of unjustified racial disparities
And acts of discrimination so blatant
That they violate basic human and civil rights
And though many want to act
As if racial profiling does not exist
There are many testimonies to the realities
Of this American problem
Is this reality or is it a nightmare?
Unfortunately, it's both for many in America
Black drivers, Black shoppers, Black walkers
Black people in general
The anger, hurt, and pain caused by the reality
That being followed while shopping
Is a not so shocking occurrence
Feeling humiliated and dehumanized
For being pulled over for unwarranted stops
Are emotions that too many people
Have been forced to suffer
From the famous author and professor
Henry Louis Gates
To the many unknown names
That have become victims in these acts
What racial profiling says about racism in America
Is that racism is very much alive
And the time is now to end racial profiling
And this form of discrimination and racism
The time is now to end
What has been a reality for many

30

I Wonder...

Sometimes I wonder
If Mama had been dealt a different hand
Would she have lived a longer life?
I wonder if Mama didn't have to quit school
To help her family after her father was hurt
Working in the coal mines
How different her life would have been
I wonder how she was affected
By having to sacrifice her future
For the future of her family
I wonder how the pressure of being an example
To her younger siblings affected her life
I wonder how different her life would have been
If her youth wasn't taken away
I wonder if she had not grown up poor
Living in the Jim Crow South
Being a victim of discrimination and racism
How much easier her life would have been
I wonder if she had not married young
And had an opportunity to get an education
And to develop a career
Would she have been granted more time
On the time clock of life
I wonder if her marriage had been better
And she had a man who was committed
A man who was faithful
And if she didn't have to be both parents
Could she have lived just a little bit longer?
I wonder what the impact was on her
Needing to work two jobs
Cleaning homes during the day and offices by night
Then rushing home to feed her children
And cleaning her own home in between
And worrying about how bills would be paid
And how food would be put on the table

And stressing over life
I really wonder what impact this had on her life
I wonder if she had been educated
On how to maintain good health
Understanding what to eat and what not to eat
Could she have avoided having diabetes
Heart problems, high blood pressure
Arthritis, and gout
I don't believe God makes mistakes
And He does things according to His will
Without needing to explain why
But sometimes, I wonder…

My Dreams

I believe in my dreams
And my dreams are me
My dreams are the blueprints of my foundation
That will one day be my legacy
My dreams allow me to be who I am designed to be
My dreams help me learn from yesterday
Appreciate today, and believe in tomorrow
My dreams help me realize the power that I have
My dreams give me confidence, courage, and hope
My dreams are never deferred
My dreams give me the vision to see my future
My dreams give me the faith to believe in my goals
My dreams are the motivation to live the life
I've always imagined
My dreams motivate me to be
Whatever I want to be
My dreams strengthen my heart, mind, and soul
My dreams are my dreams
And my dreams are me
My dreams are the fulfillment of my thoughts
My dreams are uniquely who I am
My dreams help me to stay on my chosen path
My dreams open my eyes to my future
My dreams help me believe in myself
My dreams are what make me follow my heart
My dreams help me believe in the impossible
My dreams help me believe in miracles
My dreams keep my mind open to new experiences
My dreams are the scripts to my journey
My dreams are my dreams
And my dreams are me
My dreams pick me up when I am down
My dreams light the path when the road is dark
My dreams carry me through life's challenges

My dreams help me realize nothing can stop me
My dreams change from impossible
To improbable to inevitable
My dreams remind me I will always be a dreamer
My dreams are my dreams
And my dreams are me
My dreams have become my life story
And the future chapters to come
My dreams are my life experiences
Love stories, and professional ambitions
My dreams are the manifestation
Of the inner and spiritual me
My dreams allow me to be strong
My dreams allow me to dream big
And to follow my dreams
My dreams will not allow me to stop dreaming
My dreams will take me to my destination
My dreams transform me
I cannot dismiss my dreams
To be without my dreams, is for me to not be me
Even on those days when I doubt
If my dreams will come to fruition
My dreams remain my motivation
For me to be all that I can be
My dreams are my destiny
And my dreams are me

32

The Gift of True Friendship

The gift of true friendship
Is the memories that are made and treasured!
The memories that become footprints
In the heart and mind
The memories of the bond and connection
That in its real purest form will last a lifetime
The strength of true friendship
Is the friendship's ability
To endure anything the relationship brings
To weather all storms
And to remain strong as the sun reappears
The power of true friendship
Is revealed in how people can be
In two different places
And still be close
Because of the depth and intimacy
Of a relationship that is real
The heart of true friendship
Is what is vital in holding true friendship together!
The heart manages the many emotions
That true friendship can bring
It beats to the rhythm of the joys and pains
Of friendship
And it's the spirit of the heart
That connects one heart to another
The love of true friendship
Expresses itself in the actions inspired by the heart
By the thoughts that are constant and never ending
By the emotions that bring tears of joy
During those moments of reminiscing
The gift of true friendship
Is the reminder of the importance of the bond
The reminder of the gift, strength, power
And the heart of true friendship
Is the reminder of how important it is

To hold on to true friendship
And to fight for and support true friendship
It is the love that gives us the ability to cope
When true friendship becomes distant
And seems so far away
When time puts space in between true friendship
It is the gift of true friendship that helps us realize
That true friendship isn't dying
But it is being enhanced and taken to another level
Revealing its characteristic and strength
To survive the test of time
Because the gift of true friendship
Is forever, special, and unique

33

Why Would Anyone Want to be a Nigger?

Nigger or is it Nigga!
It really doesn't make a difference
Because the origin and history of the word are the same
It is a word of disrespect and hate
And instead of being a word that is used liberally
It should be a word of embarrassment and shame
My nigger
This nigger
That nigger
Nigger, Nigger
Nigger, please
Come on, nigger
You my nigger
If you don't get any bigger
You will always be my nigger
And you want to call this a term of endearment?
Please!
Research and study the background and history
Surrounding this word of hate
And no matter how much you try
To change the meaning
It will always be a term of hate and ignorance
Regardless of any attempts to change the meaning
The word is what it is!
So I ask
"Why in the world would anyone call themselves
Or call anyone else a nigger!"
Especially those whom you claim to love
And respect
So let us eradicate this word from our vocabulary
Let us make it unacceptable to want to be a nigger
Or to call anyone else a nigger

Let us connect the past to the present
And bring understanding
That there is nothing good about this word
So I ask, "Why would anyone want to be a nigger?"

34

Daddy, Where Are You?

Daddy, where are you?
Daddy, where are you?
God had a job for you and you failed to show up
Only God can give a man an assignment
That is also a gift
Only God can give a man an opportunity
That could bless him for the rest of his life
Only God can give a man a chance
To love someone as much as He loves them
What type of man
Does not appreciate a gift from God?
What type of man does not put forth the effort
To do God's assignment?
What type of man rejects the blessings
And the gift of fatherhood?
What type of man
Would not answer a calling from God?
I ask, "What type of man?"
Sadly, we have too many men
Calling themselves men
Who do not deserve that level of respect
And we have too many men
Carrying the title of father
Simply because they donated the DNA
That made them a biological father
But I ask, "How do you have the audacity
To call yourself a father?"
A real father steps up and takes care of his own
A real father accepts his responsibilities
A real father will do what he is supposed to do
Parenting was not meant to be a solo act
And God's plan for raising a child
Wasn't for mothers to become super women
We live in a nation

With far too many fatherless children
How could any father turn his back
On someone that is a part of him?
How could any father allow his child
To be a member of the fatherless nation?
How could any father allow the intimate
Natural bond that should exist
Between a father and child to be broken?
How could any father turn his back emotionally?
How could any father turn his back financially?
A child is given as a gift from God
How could any father turn his back
On his own gift?
Being a father should be a joy, an honor
And an accepted responsibility
Marriages sometimes end
Relationships sometimes change
But the parents of a child remain the same
Children should not be blamed or used as tools
To manipulate which roles
Will be played in their lives
A child is not a pawn being sacrificed
To win a game that cannot be won
There is nothing that should cause a father
To be estranged from his gift
It is totally unacceptable for fathers
To be missing in action
Absent fathers break hearts and shatter dreams
But active fathers allow children to know
They are loved
Absent fathers create anger and bitterness
But active fathers create memories
Absent fathers cause drama that creates
A sea of emotional, psychological
And spiritual damage
But active fathers cause joy in their child's life
Absent fathers allow the wounds from their
Absence to remain unhealed
But active fathers work hard to be the father
That God designed and envisioned

God has called men to be responsible fathers
We must encourage men to embrace their
Responsibilities to be the best fathers they can be
We must end the epidemic of absentee fathers
Our children have dreams
They dream of having two loving parents
Whose chemistry makes them who they are
They dream of having family memories
That will last a lifetime
They dream that one day their dreams
Will become reality
Dreams fulfilled and shared with a loving father
No more haunting nightmares of an absent father
No more monthly checks or a court cases
But a dream that can come true
It is time to destroy the labels of deadbeat dads
Ghost dads and great pretenders
It is time to deal with the sins of the father
And to remove the shadow of a father's absence
God has called men to be responsible fathers
Children need loving, responsible fathers
Children deserve loving, responsible fathers
It is time for men
To have the courage to assume the role
Of a full-time caring and nurturing father
There is absolutely no excuse for fathers
To abandon their children
Emotionally and financially
Or who fail to be support systems to the mothers
So let us encourage all fathers
To embrace their responsibility as fathers
Because being a father is important
Daddy, where you?
Daddy, where you?
Maybe one day the response will always be:
Right here!
Daddy's right here!

35

I Am

I am what I am
A man
A son
A father
A husband
I am what I am
Strong
Committed
Educated
Real
I am what I am
A leader
A teacher
A mentor
A friend
I am what I am
Authentic
And beautifully created
To serve God
And to be the best I can be

36

Every Day I Am Reminded of Me

Every day I am reminded of me
Not just when I look in the mirror at the reflection
Not only when I look at my children
And see parts of me
From their eyes and personalities
And smiles that I see
It's hard to deny they don't remind me of me
Not just the thoughts of the many memories
That bring smiles and tears
And not just the joys and pains
That helped to develop and mold me into me
It's amazing how reflecting on the past
Reminds me of me
How the tracks of my life's path
Truly define how this is me
How when I examine the story of my journey
I am able to fully understand me
How my mind, soul, and spirit
Paint a picture of me
How the deep pulse of my heart
Reveals the life in me
How my imagination and thoughts
Show the creativity in me
How when I take a moment to reflect
I see the growth and the transformations of me
And how the ink of my pen
Will show another side of me
Every day I am truly reminded of me
From all of the gifts God has given me
To everything about me that makes me
From the inner strength and peace from within
To lifting up and encouraging everyone I can
Everything in my life has become a part of me
Yes! Every day I am reminded of me

But sadly, America has its own way
Of reminding me of me
Because of the hate, prejudice, and racism
I am constantly reminded of the state of this world
And of the divided nation I live in
Often subjected to unfair treatment
The stench from discrimination
That is always in the air
Being rejected and told no
Just because of who I am
All create a feeling of hopelessness, powerlessness
And despair
I would love to escape this reality
But unfortunately it is what it is
Painfully, this ugliness that I often face
Is also a reminder of me
And though I love the skin I'm in
My complexion and shade
The hurt and pain caused by hate and ignorance
I cannot deny
But I won't allow it to keep me down
I'm beyond asking why?
I will not hold my head low
I will always look to the sky
I will find meaning in my past
And hope for my future
There will be no tears
Because every day I will look in the mirror
And I will understand me
And how every experience of my journey
Has helped make me who I am
From the good and the bad
And the right and the wrong
Having to work twice as hard
And having to always be strong
Although my story is nowhere near complete
The reality is, there is one inescapable fact
Every day I am reminded of me

37

No Cures

It seems that the search for cures is just an illusion
In this age of pharmaceutical companies
Research foundations chasing the almighty dollar
The motivation is to search
For the next big money maker
Not for a great discovery or cure
The commitment to find
The next symptom suppressant
Makes more sense when profits are the goal
It is more important to find the next treatment
That will enslave so many people to the hope
That a cure is on the way
Than to give proof of a life saver or cure
Is it not more important to find a cure
For at least *one* of the numerous known diseases!
Telescopes have been created to study
The outer limits of the universe
Men have traveled in space
And walked on the moon
Weapons of mass destruction have been made
Organ transplants have been achieved
We even have the capability to clone life
But where is the lifeline?
Alzheimer's, cancer, diabetes, and sickle cell
Are still taking lives
AIDS, heart disease, leukemia and strokes
All continue to kill
And we won't even mention the evolution of the flu
And still we have no cures
As a matter of fact
When was the last time we cured anything?
You tell me, because I don't know!
Does life matter?
This is not just an illusion, but this is simply fact
There are no cures!

Only maintenance and treatment
A trillion dollar industry that denies cures
A health care industry unwilling
To sacrifice the profits that treatment
And medications bring
Because to them there is little profit in cure
The profits are in something given to you
To take every day for the rest of your life
But where is the search for cures?
Where is the commitment to education and
research when it comes to finding a cure?
We need to focus on what really matters
Life and the quality of life are what matter
We must be committed to finding
More than a treatment
We must be committed to finding cures
If we have the ability to solve a problem
Then we are obligated to do so
The world must not be allowed to go on
With no cures

Mama Was a Teacher

Mama was an amazing woman
Mama did not wear a cape nor could she fly
But Mama was definitely a super woman
It seemed like Mama could do anything
And with limited resources
Mama connected all of the pieces
To the puzzles of life
Mama could repair whatever was broken
With a little effort, hope and a lot of prayer
Mama could take away just about any type of pain
With a hug, a kiss, and with much love
Mama could take the worse situations
And make them all right
Mama was an advisor, cook, counselor
Doctor, nurse
And just about anything else her family needed
To function and survive
But most of all, Mama was a teacher
Mama was not accredited or certified
Nor did she have a degree
But Mama was a teacher
Mama did not go to college
And she did not have much education
But Mama knew how to teach
And she was a very good teacher
Mama didn't get her education from a university
Or her experience from a well-paying job
Mama got her wisdom from the many lessons
She learned from life
Mama's life was very seldom easy
And her journey was often very rough
But Mama learned a lot of lessons
And those lessons became lessons for her children
And for others

Mama started her day of working two jobs
Early in the morning
And often her work would not end
Until late in the evening
Mama did what she had to do
So that her family could live and survive
But Mama still found the time to teach
Mama taught me how to
Get down on my knees and pray
Mama taught me how to read my Bible every day
Mama taught me how to say
"Thank you," and "Please."
Mama taught me to do my best
No matter what I was doing
Mama taught me about right versus wrong
Mama taught me how to be strong
Mama taught me the importance of an education
Mama taught me the importance of hard work
Mama taught me about life and how life works
Mama was a teacher
And she was a very good teacher
If you would have asked Mama who she was
She would have just told you she was a mother
But if you ask me who Mama was
I would tell you that she was many things
But most of all she was a great teacher
Mama was uneducated, untrained
With no professional experience
But Mama was a teacher
Mama was the person that she was
And that person was a little bit of everything
But most of all, Mama was an awesome Mother
Because Mama was a great teacher

39

Beautiful

How did Beautiful forget that she is Beautiful?
All natural, totally organic, pure, no additives
No artificial ingredients
That was your original design, Beautiful
But what have you become?
Beautiful is what you were designed to be
Beautiful is what God made you to be
What God created and designed
Was perfectly done for what He created
What God made was good
Whether His awesome work is liked or not
It is still good
How can you not love who you are
When you were beautifully and wonderfully made?
How can you not like who you are
When you were made in God's image?
God loves you so much
That He uniquely created you
As part of His masterpiece collection
But too often Beautiful is looking in the mirror
And not loving the reflection
How did you become the beauty
That Beautiful hated?
In the age of artificial enhancements
You have lost who you are, Beautiful
Wigs, weaves, hair coloring, hair straighteners
Colored eye contacts, fake eye lashes, fake nails
Skin lighteners, and lip reductions
Do you even recognize who you are, Beautiful?
How can you hate your eyes?
How can you hate your hair?
How can you hate your complexion?
How can you hate what God created?
Why do you embrace a false image of who you are?

You are Beautiful!
What God created is perfect
What God created is good
What God created is Beautiful
Embrace your beauty, Beautiful
Stop denying who you were born to be
God loves you the way He wanted you to be
So you must love the beauty that God gave you
God does not make mistakes, Beautiful
There are no recalls when it comes to God's design
So do not be dissatisfied or unhappy
With your God-given beauty
Because God is the author of perfection
You must understand that whatever God makes
Is beautiful
He wants you to know, recognize,
And accept your beauty
He wants you to be secure in His beautiful design
If it is good enough for God
It should be good enough for you, Beautiful
Your beauty is supposed to be your glory
The truth is, whatever He blessed you with is good
Because He made it
You are Beautiful
Are you ashamed to be beautiful?
Your beauty is an intimate gift from God to you
A gift that helps to symbolize
His personal love story
So how do you not love who you are, Beautiful?
God wants all of us to be who He created us to be
It is fine to be different or to try something new
But you must not be defined or influenced
By society's false standards for your beauty
God's standard should be enough to satisfy you
Beautiful
No so-called beauty enhancers are needed
To God you are precious
To God you are special
To God you are unique
And to God, you are Beautiful

40

How Can America Have a Problem with Immigration?

How can America have a problem
With immigration
When most of America's story is
About immigration?
America has been the refuge from oppression
Persecution and violence
America is where people have come
To build a new life
America is the land of freedom
America is the land where dreams can be fulfilled
America is the land where hope becomes a reality
America has always been a nation of immigrants
From the forced immigration from Africa
To the voluntary immigration of Europeans
To Ellis Island, greeted by Lady Liberty
To those migrating from Central America and
Mexico looking for a better life
America has a long history of immigration
But it seems that America has forgotten its history
America has forgotten what has defined and made
America the nation it has become
America, once the land of a new opportunity
Has become a nation with an irrelevant history
Immigration is American history
So how can America be against immigration?
How can America become a nation
That believes it has too many immigrants
When it is a nation full of immigrants?
How can America be so opposed to immigration
Today
When immigration helped build America
Yesterday?
America, where the red, white, and blue

Were once a symbol of a new life
A symbol that provided freedom, protection
And all that comes with true democracy
Has become a nation where exclusion and
Persecution have become the new American way
America - the country that sings
"God Bless America"
Has sadly forgotten that we are all God's children
Regardless of where people may come from
America's borders should never be closed
Not to people whose lives are threatened
Not to people who are struggling to survive
Not to people who are fleeing their homelands
Not to people whose reality
Differs from Americans
How can America have a problem
With immigration
When children make a lonesome journey
To America
Because their parents fear for their survival?
How can America have a problem
With immigration
When people are risking their lives
Not for the American Dream
But for the fulfillment of the dream
For a better life?
How can America have a problem
With immigration?
America didn't shut its borders
During the forced immigration that occurred
With slavery during the country's early years
America didn't shut its borders
During its exploitation of illegal immigrants
Who were being used as cheap labor here
America didn't shut its borders
When foreign students came from all over
To study in this country
But now America has a problem with
Children escaping danger, poverty
And uncertain fates

Parents in countries like Guatemala, Honduras
Mexico and El Salvador
Are sending their children to the unknowns of
America for hope of a better life
Because they love them
But America cannot relate to their plight
Or that type of love
America needs to wake up and understand
That for many people in this world
This type of diaspora is a matter of life and death
From the founding of our nation until now
America has always recognized that
When it is a matter of life and death
America's doors have never been closed
If many Americans look into their family's history
They may find journeys similar to those
Who are now seeking to come to America
For a better life
But America didn't put them in detention centers
Or send them back to life threatening situations
America welcomed them
And helped them to change their dire situations
They became citizens of America
Helping to form and transform America
Into the great nation that it is today
We must look at the history of immigration
In America
To fully understand its impact and importance
And if we take the time
To understand immigration from a humanitarian
view
Then maybe we can live up
To what this nation is supposed to represent
And we would not have to ask
"How can America have a problem
With immigration?"

41

Footprints in the Mind:
An Act of Forgiveness

Footprints in the mind
With origins that words struggle to truly define
A struggle that battles with a piece of the mind
Holding onto anger and bitterness
That has failed to heal over time
Footprints in the mind
Of a life haunted by the pains of time
Of memories that are stuck on constant rewind
Refusing to let go of a painful period of time
Reliving a nightmare
That should have been left behind
Footprints in the mind
Unable to reconnect the links to a chain
Broken by acts of the past by someone once close
The acts from someone whose relationship
Was once was considered intimate
Has now become a damaged relationship
Footprints in the mind
Unable to forgive and forget
Knowing the right thing to do
Is to forgive and forget
But it is not always easy to forgive and forget
Sometimes life takes us to places
We really don't want to go
But we must remember
That it's only a temporary visit
An obstacle or a roadblock
During this journey called life
People will be people
And what people do sometimes hurts
But the root of the problem
Is not letting go of the pain caused by the wrong
The root of the problem

Is holding onto the pain
That often affects one's emotional, psychological
And even physical well being
Crippling one's ability to be whole
Happiness, joy, and love of life are damaged
By an inability to let go of the past
And the hurt it brought
Praying for strength that maybe tomorrow
Will bring joy back to a life
That once had inner peace
An inner peace on this journey called life
Reaching back into the past and forgiving
So that one can again live a life of moving forward
Of being the person that one was designed to be
Footprints in the mind
In need of an act of forgiveness
Not a second chance
But forgiveness
So that one can move on with life
No longer being enslaved to the negative thoughts
No longer a prisoner to an act of deception
Ugliness
Unfaithfulness
Wrong doing
One can forgive
One must forgive
Forgiveness will set one free
Forgiving the inner damage caused by another
Forgiving so the past will no longer hurt
Forgiving so that one can live again
Forgiving so the footprints in the mind
Can be washed away by acts of forgiveness
And replaced with new footprints
Footprints of positive life experiences
Even when the forgiveness isn't deserved
Footprints in the mind

42
I Am Able to Smile

I sometimes shake my head when I think about
What I thought my life would be
Compared to what it has become
I sometimes laugh when I think about
The many things I have done
That I said I would never do
I sometimes cry when I remember
The painful mistakes that I have made
And the many hurtful lessons that I had to endure
I sometimes meditate on those learned lessons
That have made me a bit stronger and a bit wiser
I sometimes pray that today
Won't be like yesterday
And that tomorrow
Will begin many wonderful days
I sometimes smile about what my life has become
And though all of my days haven't been perfect
And life sometimes brought challenges
Disappointments, and tough times
Life has been good
And I am able to smile

What If?

What if you had the ability to plan a dream?
Would you live out your dreams
Or would the fears of your desires hold you back?
What if the perfect dream could really come true?
Would you be brave enough to make a memory
And allow that dream
To become a special part of you?
What if you could control each day?
Would each day be perfect
Or would you just let each day do
Whatever it will do?
What if you could change the past
And predict the future?
Would you control your life
Or would you let life bring what it brings?
What if you had the ability to go back in time
And correct past mistakes?
Would you make that journey to change the past
Or would you leave the past alone
And be thankful for the lessons learned?
What if you could be totally free?
Would you liberate yourself
Or be in mental bondage to your inner thoughts?
What if yesterday could be today?
Would you change anything
Or would life remain the same?
What if the secrets of your heart
Could be revealed?
What story would your heart tell?
And would you be brave enough to share?
What if your heart could be stolen?
What type of hostage would you be?
Would you be hostile and fight to be free?
What if you could go anywhere?

Where would your destination be?
Would you stay where you are
Or would you travel the world to see?
What if you could have one wish?
What would that wish be?
Would it be something intimate?
What if opportunity was staring you in the face?
Would you recognize it
Or would you let it pass you by?
What if one of your thoughts was stolen?
What would the thought reveal?
What if you could be whatever you wanted?
Would you allow it?
What if?

44

I Must Say Thank You

From our introduction, you were there for me
Giving me the perfect picture
When my eyes opened for the very first time
Making sure I knew I was loved from my beginning
Defining what true love was supposed to be
Teaching me my first words
Helping me take my first steps
Caring for me like no other could
Directing and guiding me in the ways I should go
Encouraging me to be all that I could be
Lifting me up when I was down
Protecting me from all harm
Supporting me in those things I desired to do
Always believing in me
Never doubting my ability to succeed
Teaching me lessons that would last a lifetime
Showing me how I could reach my full potential
No doubt
You took your God-given assignment seriously
An assignment you would have failed
If not for your faith in your Heavenly Father
If not for the love you had
For a special gift from God
A love so strong and so deep
That it became easy to put the gift above yourself
Never looking to be lifted up, praised, or rewarded
Never complaining about this assignment
Or needing to do it alone
Never allowing the needs for the gift to not be met
And even though lacking this
And lacking that came often
You always found a way to address each need
You taught the lesson that even in need
Blessings flowed
You were the perfect example

Of how to juggle so many roles
Yet not look stressed
You knew how to make something out of nothing
And everything you made was always special
It is amazing how someone with so little
Could do so much
From my beginning to your end
You were there for me
As I was a gift to you, you were also a gift to me
A mentor, provider, teacher, trainer
And most of all a mother
You didn't have to take your assignment seriously
But you did and because you did
I am who I am today
The assignment wasn't always easy
But you never gave up
The assignment brought many joys and many tears
The assignment taught us both many lessons
The assignment created a bond
That revealed how perfect God's plan was for us
And as always
He knew what He was doing
When He assigned us to each other
Because we were a perfect match
God knew your heart
And how deeply you would love
God knew you would be committed
To the high calling of your assignment
God knew you could handle this solo act so well
That you could have won an Oscar
It is amazing how you and so many women
Not only stepped up to the challenge
Of doing what was designed for two people
But did it so well
I am so thankful for your commitment and love
You were not only a mother for me
But also a mother for many
A role model in the community
An example of how it takes a village to raise a child
It seemed like you were everyone's mother

And in a fatherless community like ours
It was a necessity
Because being a mother with no father around
Wasn't easy
You were committed to helping
And supporting other mothers
Whenever and however you could
You understood the importance
Of being there for others
And allowing others to be there for you
You understood that doing it alone
Didn't necessarily have to mean
That you were alone
And even when the tough times of life would arrive
You never felt alone
Because most of all
You always knew that God was always with you
So I'm thankful to God
For such an amazing, strong, and wonderful gift
Whose commitment to her assignment
Developed me into who I am today!
You weren't perfect
And you probably made some mistakes
But all I know is you were the best mother for me
And because of that
I must say thank you

45

This Heart of Mine

This heart of mine defines who I am
Through all of my joys and through all of my pains
My heart is the vault that guards
My emotions and feelings
Protecting me from anything and everything
This heart of mine is what makes me better today
Than I was yesterday
Helping me to learn from the days of my past
Whether those days were good or bad
My heart has treated each day as a life lesson
Growing and learning from my many experiences
Growing and learning from my many relationships
Helping me to prepare for the days of my future
The beats of my heart are the rhythms
That make me stronger
My heart is the diary that knows my story
Hiding and protecting my most intimate thoughts
My heart pumps the blood
That is the source of my inner strength
My heart is full of love and passion
My heart is totally honest and transparent with me
The instinct of my heart
Picks up what my eyes will miss
Often helping me to do what is right for me
This heart of mine is very precious
But this heart of mine is also fragile
And even though my heart guards my emotions
And guards my feelings
I am still often vulnerable to hurt and pain
My heart has been beaten, broken
And disappointed
My heart has persevered through many battles
And though my heart is sometimes filled with pain
This heart of mine is still beating

My heart heals and allows me
To experience happiness
My heart heals and allows me to experience joy
My heart comforts me
In the silence of sleepless nights
My heart sometimes cries in solitude
But sometimes this heart of mine sings in the rain
My heart allows me
To live this life of mine to the fullest
Living, laughing, loving, and enjoying life
No one knows me like this heart of mine
My heart knows my strengths and my weaknesses
My heart knows my dreams and my fears
My heart knows all of my thoughts
My heart knows me
I thank God every day
For giving me this heart of mine

46

No More Promises

"My country tis of thee
Sweet land of liberty
Of thee I sing
Land where my Fathers died
Land of the pilgrim's pride
From every mountain side
Let freedom ring!"

As we approach another four years
Of political drama - American style
As usual, we must prepare ourselves
For what seems like a television mini-series
Called "Election Time"
As the Republican Party tries to justify
Why they couldn't and wouldn't
Support the President or the Democratic Party
Over the past four years
And the Democratic Party blames their inability
To do all they wanted to do over the past four years
On the Republican Party
America has become tired
Tired of the finger pointing and verbal attacks
Tired of the commercials laden with half-truths
Or in many cases with no truth at all
America has become a divided nation
And America continues
To be a victim of broken promises
So please! No more promises America
As history speaks
And the present gives us examples
Of so many broken promises
How much more can the heart of a nation take?
Promises of a better America
Promises of a new day

Promises of better education
Promises of a better future for our young people
Promises of more jobs, less taxes
And of ending war
Promises of fixing all of the nation's problems
Promises that we won't forget
About the poor and elderly
Promises that we won't forget
About all of the war troops coming home
Changed mentally and physically
Promises of this and promises of that
But please, no more unfulfilled promises
No more of the political games
Played by the Democrats and the Republicans
Or played by the conservatives and liberals
Do any of these groups really care about America?
Or are they just groups
Pushing their own agendas?
I guess we need a new Emancipation Proclamation
Because it feels like we are slaves
To this political system
Yesterday is gone, today is almost over
And the thoughts about tomorrow are scary
So no more promises
Because the words being preached
Just do not mean a whole lot these days
The many promises have just become empty words
Promises so broken we cannot even distinguish
Between the then and the now
It seems the before and the after an election
Really have a strong resemblance to each other
As we continue to be pawns
In the chess game of broken promises
And as our nation remains angry and confused
Let's have no more lies
No more manipulation of the facts
No more refusals to support our elected officials
Regardless of their political affiliations
Let's have no more promises if they cannot be kept
Let's not promise words that will fail

Let's not promise words
That will eventually reveal a lie
Let's not promise words
That will take us back in time
To remind us of the past broken promises
Let today be the beginning of something new
If you must make a promise
Promise a day when we will no longer be played
Like 88 keys
By those chasing political dreams
Promise me a day when our politicians
Will say what they mean and mean what they say
Promise me a day
When we can believe in the American dream
Promise me a day when the economic divide
Between the haves and the have-nots
Is not as wide as our oceans
Promise me a day
When we won't have to fight for justice
Promise me a day
That will not be another chapter
Of America attempting to hold on
To pieces of its ugly past
Promise me a day
When there will be unity in America
Promise me we will work together
To make a difference
And to put forth effort
To change America for the better
And if this is just too much to ask or it is not possible
Then please do not make any more promises

"My country tis of thee
Sweet land of liberty
Of thee I sing
Land where my Fathers died
Land of the pilgrim's pride
From every mountain side
Let freedom ring!"

47

Love and Friendship

Some people look at love
The way they look at friendship
Some people look at friendship
The way they look at love
They look at them as being one in the same
Not revealing any great differences
Between the characteristics
Of these two unique practices
Some people don't realize
That there is a distinction
Between these two special ways
Of intimately connecting
Love is love and friendship is friendship
And every once in a while
They cross the line that separates them
Attempting to become one
Sometimes successfully and sometimes failing
To maintain the love or friendship
The act of love
When it is real
Is so intense and powerful
That it creates a sense of oneness with another
The act of friendship
When it is real
Is so strong
That it creates an enduring bond
Between two uniting forces
Both can be very special nouns
When they're honored and respected
Love and friendship
Can become deep personal relationships
That will exhibit powerful actions
And strong feelings
That embrace their true meanings

Love and friendship
Can also cause frustration and damage the heart
Love and friendship should be positive, alive
And active
But unfortunately
They can evolve into negative actions
That lead to the death of love and friendship
Because some people fail to realize
The depth of emotions
That separate the two from each other
Some people fail to realize
That even though one can love
And also have friendship
It doesn't mean that one should de-emphasize
The depth, faithfulness, and intimacy of love
Or the commitment and honesty of friendship
To some people love and friendship
Mean everything
To some people love and friendship
Mean very little at all
To some people love and friendship
Bring joy
To some people love and friendship
Bring hurt and pain
To some people love and friendship
Are like the music of a beautiful melody
To some people love and friendship
Are like the sounds of one mourning
To some people love and friendship
Are the excitement that comes with a new day
To some people love and friendship
Are the drama that just won't go away
If love and friendship are real
Then their worth should be priceless
There should be total commitment
And total dedication to the love and friendship
And if they are truly real
Then they are worth fighting for
Both love and friendship

48

Sometimes I Just Need to Get Away

Maybe I will choose the Caribbean
And its clear blue sea as far as the eyes can see
With its beautiful white sand beaches
And all of its different unique island cultures
Maybe a little bit of that Calypso and Reggae music
Would be perfect for me
Maybe I will choose the Blue Ridge Mountains
With the wide range of colors
Being revealed as the seasons change
Hiking some of the many trails
And eating mountain-grown pecans
In this peaceful sanctuary
Maybe that is just what I need
Maybe I will choose the Big Apple
The city that never goes to sleep
Full of activities, excitement, and energy
Maybe that would be all that I need
To help me to get back to being me
Maybe I will choose the Big Easy
With all of the different types of music
That could relax my soul
And the good tasting food
That would take me on a delectable adventure
Maybe that should be my destination
Maybe I will choose Toronto, Canada
One of the most beautiful cities in the world
Experiencing its international flavor
And its diverse atmosphere
That makes it so unique
Maybe crossing the border
Is where you will find me
Every once in a while I just need to get away
Away from home

Away from work
Away from the demands and responsibilities
That I've come to know oh, so well
Every once in a while I just need to get away
From life
And the problems that life sometimes brings
Every once in a while I need moments
To escape from reality
And to find reconciliation with myself
Reconnecting with the self that I once knew
In what has become the daily routines of life
Rediscovering the dreams
That became the motivation for life
Recapturing the love for self and life
Reflecting on where I should be in life
And where I should be going in life
Sometimes I just need to get away
On a therapeutic journey
A journey to deal with the bad
A journey to enjoy the good about my life
A journey to deal with who should be in my life
A journey to deal with who shouldn't be in my life
A journey to rest my body, mind, and soul
A journey to find inner peace
Every once in a while I need to just get away
So that I can be the best me that I can be
It could be some place near or someplace far away
It could be my secret place
Or a place I choose to share
With family and friends
But it is my personal get away
And sometimes that is all I need
It doesn't matter if it is in the mountains
Or at the ocean
It doesn't matter if I am in a big city
Or a foreign country
It doesn't get any better
Than getting away for a while and enjoying life
Because sometimes
I just need to get away

Sometimes I'm Rhythm and Sometimes I'm Blues

Sometimes I'm rhythm and sometimes I'm blues
Some days I'm happy
And some days I'm confused
Some days I'm smiling
And some days I'm not
Some days I'm weak
And some days I'm strong
Because sometimes I'm rhythm
And sometimes I'm blues
Sometimes there's sunshine
And sometimes there's rain
Sometimes I have days that I just can't explain
Sometimes there's joy
And sometimes there's pain
And sometimes I feel like I'm going insane
Sometimes there's laughter
And sometimes there are tears
Because sometimes I'm rhythm
And sometimes I'm blues
Sometimes I do right
And sometimes I do wrong
Sometimes I'm proud of who I am
And sometimes I'm afraid to be alone
Sometimes I'm brave
And sometimes I'm not
Sometimes you see the fear in me more than not
Sometimes I have a lot to say
And sometimes I have no words at all
Sometimes I won't pick up the phone
Because sometimes I'm rhythm
And sometimes I'm blues
Enjoying my highs
And dealing with my lows

Learning how to put them together
And creating what they call "soul"
Taking away the sometimes
And creating something whole
Realizing that my journey makes me who I am
And my life experiences make me whole
Both the good and the bad
And the sun and the rain
Yes!
Sometimes I'm rhythm and sometimes I'm blues

50

The Dash

The dash is more than a small line
Carved into a granite tombstone
Separating two dates
The dash is more than a line trapped
Between the beginning and the end
Of a life-long journey
The dash is a representation of the many chapters
That tell the story of a lifetime
The dash represents each year of life
From its beginning to the end
The dash is a look at what life has been
The dash is how our lives define us
We must understand that we all have a dash
The dash is what God would like us to focus on
As we strive to be who He has designed us to be
The dash is something we should think about daily
Because during each day of our lives
We add a little more to the dash
That represents how we are living this life
We should look at the dash as if it is a mirror
Just as a mirror gives a reflection
Of the image of the person looking in
So the dash reflects who we are
The dash is the portrait of the person we are
The person we were
And the person we never became in life
The dash stands for every second, minute, hour
And day that we are alive
The dash symbolizes our entire lifetime
The highs and the lows
The joys and the pains
The successes and the failures
The dash reveals when we were extraordinary
And when we were ordinary

And the times when we failed to even try
The dash tells if our life has been fulfilled
Or unfulfilled
The dash also represents how our life was lived
The dash is like a question mark asking
"What does your life story say about you?"
The dash is our legacy
From the time we were born till the time we die
The dash is the legacy that we will leave behind
When the final chapter of life ends
The dash is the legacy that we will be remembered
The dash defines our legacy
The dash reveals the periods in life
When we were connected to God
And those periods in life
When we were disconnected from God
The dash reminds us of those times
When we could only say, "Thank you Lord."
The dash reminds us
That our journey is not all about us
But it is truly about glorifying Him
Who gave us this life
The dash is a personal inventory
Of self-accountability
The dash reveals the intimacies of our lives
The dash reveals our perfections
And the dash reveals our imperfections
The dash reveals our fears and the tears
The dash reveals our hurt and pain
The dash shows the application
From the many lessons that life has taught us
The dash hopefully will be the definition
Of what life should become
When we look at the dash
We don't always see how long the dash truly is
It is not easy thinking of life as a dash
No one knows how long their dash will be
But we can all determine what our dash will reveal
The dash should cause us to ask ourselves
"Who am I and what is my purpose?"

The dash should make us look at the good
And the bad in the person we are
The dash should make us consider our dash
And ask, "What does my dash say about my life
My legacy, and who I am?"
Because the dash is much more than a mark
Squeezed in between two dates
The dash is who we truly are

51

Those Bus Rides

Mama never learned how to drive
But Mama could take you all over the city
On the bus
Mama could go here, there or just about anywhere
On those bus rides
Mama knew the city well
And her familiarity with the city
Came from her daily bus rides
Mama went everywhere on the bus
Mama would get up early in the morning
To catch the bus to work
She worked hard to clean the offices
At her second job
So she could catch the last bus
Running home each night
Mama would catch the bus to go to church
Then walk several blocks from the bus stop
Up a hill to worship the God she loved
Mama would catch the bus to go shopping
The bus drivers often stopped the bus
Right in front of her home
Instead of the bus stop
So she would not have to carry her bags
A block up the street to her home
Mama traveled on the bus like she was a dignitary
Being chauffeured around the city
Every bus driver knew her
And she knew each of them
Mama not only knew them
But she cared about them
She would often ask them about their families
And if there was anything she could pray for them
Mama knew so many people
And many of those people she met

Were on those bus rides
Many people who sat with Mama while riding
Would get off the bus with a new friend
Mama enjoyed her bus rides
She believed that every time she got on a bus
It was an opportunity to touch a life
The bus rides were often down time for Mama
A time when she could meditate on her thoughts
The bus rides were times
When Mama heard God's voice
And when she connected with her Heavenly Father
The bus rides became a part
Of her personal ministry
She often shared the good news of the gospel
And her love for her Lord and Savior Jesus Christ
The bus rides not only revealed who Mama was
And her love for life and others
But the rides also revealed God's love for us
The bus rides became life lessons for anyone
Who just happened to be sitting near Mama
Those who rode the bus with Mama
Often got off the bus
With a unique connection to her
Mama turned many short rides on the bus
Into memories and lessons that lasted a lifetime
Those bus rides were times when Mama
Spent precious time with her grandchildren
Often sharing with them who and whose they were
Mama used those bus rides
To tell them about their journey
And how they could sit anywhere on the bus
Because of that journey
Those bus rides were the time that Mama
Would share her own personal story
It was also the time that Mama would take
To learn who her grandchildren were
But most of all, those bus rides
Were times Mama would spend with her only son
Teaching him everything she knew about life
The bus rides were precious and priceless

Those bus rides were Mama's way of showing
How abundant life can truly be
So even though Mama did not have a lot of money
Those bus rides allowed Mama
To do what Mama did best
And that was to share some of that Mama's love
And it was the sharing of her love
That made those bus rides very special

52

Smile

Too often we underestimate the power of a smile
A smile is the sunshine that lights a beautiful day
A smile is a simple act
That can change any day into a great day
A smile is the positive energy
That inspires a difference
A smile is the universal greeting
That can brighten a day
For some people a smile may be hard to come by
Maybe they are having a bad day
We never know what is going on
In the lives of people whose paths we cross
A smile may be just what they need
Every day we have opportunities
To bring joy into someone's life with a smile
Every day we have opportunities
To cheer and lift someone up with the flashing of a smile
Every day we have the opportunity
To witness the amazing power of a smile
One smile can brighten the darkest day
A simple smile can be just as strong
As an act of caring, kind words
Or being a good listener
A smile is the most inexpensive gift you can give
Smiling is contagious and when you give a smile
You will often receive a smile in return
Every time you smile at someone
It is a positive action
A way of speaking without speaking
An expression that says so much
With so little effort
A smile is encouraging, therapeutic, and uplifting
A smile is an act of love

One smile can make all the difference in the world
A smile has the power to be infectious
We should start every day with a smile
And wait for the responses to our smiles
A smile at the right moment
May be the turning point for someone
Who is struggling in life
We should never miss an opportunity to smile
Or to put a smile on someone's face
Because it may be the only opportunity
For them to smile
A smile is much more than a simple act
One we often take for granted
A smile is much more
Than the expression of happiness
That appears across our faces
A smile should grace our face every day
Because life is too short not to smile
Smiling is a symbol of our strength
And we give strength
When we put a smile on someone's face
A smile is a beautiful way to start each day
We must always remember that smiling matters
And we must never underestimate
The power of a smile

53

We Must Be Our Brother's Keeper

Are we our Brother's keeper?
When our Brother is down and cannot get up
Then yes!
We must be our Brother's keeper
When our Brother is lacking inner-strength
Then yes!
We must be our Brother's keeper
When our Brother is sick and in pain
Then yes!
We must be our Brother's keeper
When our Brother cannot escape past mistakes
Then yes!
We must be our Brother's keeper
When our Brother's world seems upside down
Then yes!
We must be our Brother's keeper
When our Brother is in need of encouraging words
Then yes!
We must be our Brother's keeper
When our Brother cannot find any peace of mind
Then yes!
We must be our Brother's keeper
When our Brother's head is hanging low
Then yes!
We must be our Brother's keeper
When our Brother's confidence is down
Then yes!
We must be our Brother's keeper
When our Brother is not doing right
Then yes!
We must be our Brother's keeper
When our Brother needs guidance and direction
Then yes!
We must be our Brother's keeper
When our Brother has lost his joy

Then yes!
We must be our Brother's keeper
When our Brother's light has lost its shine
Then yes!
We must be our Brother's keeper
When our Brother experiences injustice
Then yes!
We must be our Brother's keeper
When for our Brother, innocence doesn't matter
Then yes!
We must be our Brother's keeper
When the world is unsympathetic
To our Brother's plight
Then yes!
We must be our Brother's keeper
When our Brother is caught in the eye of the storm
Then yes!
We must be our Brother's keeper
When our Brother sees no light
At the end of the tunnel
Then yes!
We must be our Brother's keeper
When our Brother does not feel optimistic
Then yes!
We must be our Brother's keeper
We must be part of the solution
To our Brother's problem
So yes!
We must be our Brother's keeper

54

The Kitchen Table

During many of the years of her life
The kitchen table had become the place
That often revealed her strengths and weaknesses
The kitchen table daily symbolized her joys
The kitchen table daily symbolized her pains
The kitchen table was a place of comfort
And relaxation
But the kitchen table was also a place of escape
To where she meditated on her daily thoughts
The kitchen table was where you often found her
Dealing with the struggles of everyday life
The kitchen table was where you found her
Early in the morning, before anyone would be up
Or late into the night, after everyone was asleep
The kitchen table had become her sanctuary
Where she often would meditate
And pray for the guidance from God
That would lead her through another day
The kitchen table was where she began her days
With her daily devotional
And fellowship with the Lord
The kitchen table was where her nights
Often ended in constant prayer
And where her Bible was often found
Left open to her favorite passages
The kitchen table was her place of refuge
During the limited amount of time she was granted
The kitchen table became a big part
Of defining who she was
For her, the kitchen table was like a recliner
A place for rest
And a much needed time-out after the long days
That the labor that working two jobs would bring
And a place where she sat and gathered the energy

To make sure that the everyday duties
And needs of her home were still met
The kitchen table was her place to daydream
Manage, plan and think
The kitchen table was her office and her respite
The kitchen table was where she tried
To connect the dots to this puzzle called life
The kitchen table was where she dealt
With the gloom that had always seemed ride her
The kitchen table was where she had overcome
Wishing her dreams would become reality
To hoping and praying that her dreams
Would simply become possibilities
The kitchen table was more
Than a family gathering place
And where meals were eaten
The kitchen table was the place
Where the unpaid bills were often spread
Where counseling sessions were held
And where personal self-inventories were done
The kitchen table was often the place of silence
The kitchen table was often the place
Of blank stares
The kitchen table was sometimes that best friend
In whom she would confide her fears and worries
The kitchen table were the ears
That always listened
The kitchen table was the place
Often flooded by her tears
Caused by the constant reminders of her reality
The kitchen table was treated like it understood
All of her complexities, moods, and pains
Often, looking out of the window
From the kitchen table
Gave her the only glimpses of sunshine
She would see
The rays from the sunshine
Highlighted certain aspects
During different points of her life
The sunshine that gave her the strength

To make needed paradigm shifts
That would grant her some peace of mind
The kitchen table helped her realize
That life wasn't always a blind descent to nowhere
The kitchen table helped her realize
That reality didn't always have to be broken
And that she didn't always have to be bound
By the chains of confusion, frustration
And suffering
While sitting at the kitchen table
She had developed a way to maintain order
Before it became a disorder
The kitchen table
Was where she learned from mistakes
And taught herself to remain conscious
Of the lines she knew she couldn't cross
Fully maintaining the presence of mind
That there was no room for compromise
If she was going to maintain any of her joy
The kitchen table
Was where she opened her book of life
And turned the many pages
That made up chapter after chapter
She would cry, laugh, and smile
About what her life had been
Being able to totally appreciate the beauty
Of the many seasons of her life
And being able to fully embrace
Her life's joys and pains
No matter what the circumstances were
Because through it all
She knew she was still very blessed
Publically, she always hid
The not so good about her life
With a smile and a hug
And the only ones who knew the whole story
Were the Lord and the kitchen table

55

Daddy Was a Good Man

Daddy was a good man
Wherever Daddy was
His presence demanded attention
The community embraced him
And the streets loved him
He was confident, proud, and strong
To many in the community
He was the picture of what a man should be
He went to work every day
And was always willing to help someone in need
During a time when things weren't fair
For a Black man
Daddy was usually treated well and with respect
Daddy loved sports
And rarely missed big sporting events
Daddy loved to fish
And could sit on the banks of the river all day
Daddy supported his friends
And protected his family
And most of all
Daddy loved his seed like he loved himself
Daddy was a good man
But unfortunately
Daddy did not fully understand his role as a father
Because Daddy wasn't always there
It wasn't that Daddy didn't love being a father
Because knowing
That there were people in the world
Who were a part of him made him very proud
But Daddy really didn't know *how* to be a father
Daddy knew how to have a good time
Daddy knew how to chase women
Daddy knew how to gamble
Daddy knew how to hold his liquor

Daddy knew how to run the streets
And Daddy knew how
To put a foot in someone's behind
But Daddy struggled
To be the best Daddy he could be
Daddy didn't have a good daddy himself
Daddy didn't have a mentor
Daddy didn't have a role model
Daddy didn't have a manual
On how to be a good Daddy
All Daddy had was what Daddy knew
And that was that he loved his children
And he would be the best Daddy he knew how to be
Despite his battles with his personal demons
If money was needed, he provided what he had
If his children needed anything
He did his best to get it
If his children wanted to go somewhere
He took them
And he seldom hit his children
Because in his mind
It would change their view of him as a good Daddy
The picture they saw of him meant a lot to him
Daddy was a good man
He believed the parenting of his children
Should be done by Mom
He believed the disciplining of his children
Should be done by Mom
He believed that just about everything
Should be done by Mom
And thank God his children had a strong mom
A woman who couldn't maintain his faithfulness
But a woman he knew he could count on
To take care of his children
He wasn't perfect and he never claimed to be
He made many mistakes
And had many shortcomings
He was dealt a great hand
But sadly he just didn't know how to play the game
He had an idea of would it took to be a man

But he struggled when it came to being a father
He didn't understand
That in order to be a good man
He had to also be a good father
He wasn't a deadbeat Daddy
He wasn't the "I don't care" type of Daddy
Because he cared and loved his children very much
He was just a man
Who didn't know how to be a good Daddy
But Daddy was a good man

56

I Love You

I love you
I love you deeper than anyone will ever know
I love you during your good and bad times
I love you for who you are
And for who you are striving to be
I love the goodness in you
And your efforts to be the best person you can be
I love your heart and your desire to help others
I love how you pick up others when they are down
I love you
I love you during your hurts and pains
I love you when your shortcomings are high
And your struggles have you low
I love you in your imperfections
I love you when you feel all alone
I love you when it seems like no one else cares
I love you
I love you because I believe in you
I love you because I know you
I love you because we are one
I love you because you have it in you to be special
I love you because I can see your future
I love you because where you go
I will be there too
I love you
I must always remember to let you know I love you
Because we are one
Sometimes I have to tell myself, "I love you"
Because if I don't love myself, who will?
And how can anyone love me
If I don't know how to love myself
And if I don't show by example
How I'm to be loved?
So today I say to myself, "I love you."

57

Knowing What I Know Now

Knowing what I know now
Would I change anything?
Would I go back in time and do things differently?
With knowledge of my past
Would I choose to be a time traveler?
And go back to troubleshoot and fix mistakes
And take advantage of missed opportunities
And advise myself whether to go left or right
And to do this and not to do that
In my life story
Should I take that walk down memory lane
And revisit the highs and lows
And the joys and pains of my life?
Should I examine and review what has made me?
Should I closely study my past
To fully understand its impact
On my present and future?
Should I look at all of the good and all of the bad
The achievements and the failures
The dreams fulfilled and the regrets?
Should I remember the people
Who played a positive role
And those people
Who brought confusion, hurt, and pain?
Knowing what I know now
Would I change who I am
Or would I accept my past
And learn from my life experiences
Would I be smarter, wiser
And use better judgment?
Would I make better choices
Regarding those in my life?
Would I avoid some relationships?
Would I attempt to enter into others?

Would I refuse to be bound
By the chains of my mistakes?
Would I remember to smile and laugh?
Would I remember to enjoy life to the fullest?
And remember that I will never be perfect?
Knowing what I know now
I would always thank God every day for who I am
Because no matter how bad things were
God was always with me
Knowing what I know now
I would trust in the Lord
And invite God into all areas of my life
A look back into my past would show me
How life's journey has helped
To strengthen my faith
And has helped me to understand that God is able
Even when it felt like the walls were caving in
And my world was turning upside down
God has always been with me
Knowing what I know now
Would give me reason to believe
To believe in myself and in my future
Knowing what I know now
Would teach me to appreciate and love who I am
It would teach me to enjoy life
And to not throw it away
It would teach me to be thankful
For my many blessings
Knowing what I know now

In the Beginning, God Created Just a Man

**In the beginning
When God created the world
He created a man
He wasn't African-American, Black, Negro
Colored or Nubian
He wasn't identified by the color of his skin
Or by a tribe or country
He wasn't a nigger, nigga
Or any other derogatory name
Or so-called term of endearment
In the beginning
God created just a man**

59

I Often Find My Days Too Short

I often find my days too short
To do all of the things I had planned to do
I often find my days too short
To entertain all of my thoughts
I often find my days too short
To talk to everyone I would like to talk with
I often find my days too short
To visit those friends I would like to see
I often find my days too short
To do what should be a priority in my life
I often find my days too short
To be all that I can be
I often find my days too short
To reach anywhere near my full potential
I often find my days too short
To make my dreams and goals a reality
I often find my days too short
To sort out all of its issues
I often find my days too short
To be used by God
I often find my days too short
To be a blessing to others
I often find my days too short
To be the man that God has designed me to be
I often find my days too short
To spend time with God
And unfortunately I often make my days too short
To honor and worship God
All I want are days that will allow me
To be everything I want to be
And to do everything I want to do
All I want is for my days to be complete
But I must say, I often find my days too short

60

Through Your Eyes

Through your eyes
I saw joy
I saw pain
I saw the excitement from the joy
I saw the scars from the pain
Through your eyes
I saw your experiences from life
And how those experiences
Made you who you were
Through your eyes
I saw your faith
I saw your inner beauty
I saw your hope
I saw your strength
Through your eyes
I saw the love in you
I saw the meaning of love
I saw your ability to give love
I saw your need for love and to be loved
I saw how much love was in you
Through your eyes
I saw perfect days
And I saw storms
But after the storms
Through your eyes
I saw the strong survivor that you were
Through your eyes
I saw you
I truly saw my mother

61

What if the World Was Perfect?

What if the world was perfect
And all great dreams could come true
What if every day was sunny
And the rain was just God thinking about you
What if there were only joys
And never any pain
What if the world was about helping those in need
And so much focus wasn't on personal gain
What if the world was different
And didn't seem so insane
Maybe the world would have more joy
And wouldn't have so much pain
What if everyone cared about one another
And love was all we knew
Just imagine how the world would be
If this were only true
What if there was peace in the world
And the fighting would be no more
What if racism didn't exist anymore
What if everyone cared about one another
Lending a helping hand and more
Being there for one another
Recognizing when someone is in need for sure
What if everyone was happy
And sad days didn't exist anymore
A smile on everyone's face would shine
And only the sky was blue
What if there was no crime, hunger, or violence
How beautiful the world would be
With everyone getting along
What a beautiful rainbow you would see
There would be no time for conflict and fighting
And only the sharing of love there would be
What if there was true change in the world

A change we all could believe in and see
What if this was truly the world
As God designed it to be
It is a shame that God's design
Has to be viewed as unique and extraordinary
So let's make a commitment to do His will
So the world is no longer a disgrace
If we put God first in what we do
"What if" would have no place

Life is What We Make of It

It is often said life is what we make of it
We spend much of our early life
Dreaming of what we would like our life to be
And then we spend the rest of our life
Trying to make those dreams come true
Dreams of living life to the fullest
Dreams of having the perfect life
Dreams of having the perfect job
Dreams of having the perfect love
Sometimes dreams are fulfilled
And they become that perfect reality
And sometimes those dreams we had envisioned
Remain unfulfilled
And take us down roads
We never thought we'd travel
And introduce us to experiences
We never imagined
But dreams fulfilled or unfulfilled do not mean
Life cannot be all it can be
Because life is what life is
And life is what we make of it
Life doesn't have to be so complicated and deep
Life is simply living and not existing
Enjoying every moment
And everything that life has to offer
And learning from the many lessons
That life will teach
A combination of the joys and pains we experience
But even with the not so good life experiences
Life is what we make of it
We must understand there is chemistry
With the many characteristics of life
We must realize that even work and play
Can be one in the same

We should do one as easily as the other
Both work and play should bring comfort and joy
We should do both with commitment, passion
And a seriousness that defines who we are
In work and play, we should see what makes us
Who we are
And most of all
We should see a passion for what we do
Whatever we do should be a reflection of us
Whether we are working or playing
A true picture of us should be revealed
We should find who we are in all that we do
And never allow anything
To compromise who we are
We should focus on
Finding satisfaction in what we do
And through a satisfaction in all that we do
We can learn to reach our full potential
And then we will realize
That life is what we make of it

Fifty Years Later: An Anniversary

An anniversary is a special time of celebration
A time of commemoration
Anniversaries are the times we remember
The unions of those who are close and special to us
They are the dates of events with great significance
Events that made marks in the chapters of history
Anniversaries are usually times to recognize
The contributions and influences
That have become footprints in our minds
Whether celebrating a 50-year marriage
Or remembering the date of a great past event
Anniversaries are usually very special
Anniversaries are a time of honoring
And paying respect
A time when we often look back
For a proper perspective when looking forward
A time when we focus on remembering those
Who have helped to impact our journey
But sometimes anniversaries can be a bittersweet
Time of celebration and commemoration
A time when we are reminded of America's past
The 50th anniversary
Of the 1963 March on Washington
But 50 years later how can we truly celebrate
Without realizing what was true then
Is still true today
After 50 years
Who would have thought the spirit of equality
Freedom and justice would still be elusive?
On August 28, 1963
On the steps of the Lincoln Memorial
There was a plea for a better America
During some of America's most unjust times
A diverse America came together

A turning point in American history
A gathering that was not a protest in anger
But rather a stance for a better America
A gathering that was not only about blacks
In America
But it was a gathering that was about
All American people
A moment in history that was much bigger
Than a King
Much larger than a dream
Fifty years ago
The many faces of America came together
To make a statement
That America needed to change
Fifty years ago
The many faces of America demanded
Jobs and freedom
Fifty years ago
The many faces of America came together
To say there was no place for discrimination
Disenfranchisement, inequality
Injustice or racism in America
Fifty years ago
Americans spent a day soul searching
But fifty years later
The essence of the times remains unchanged
And the dream is still not a reality
America still has poor people
America still has racism
America still has poor educational systems
America still has high unemployment
America is still a nation divided between the races
Divided between the haves and the have-nots
Fifty years later
America has a black President in the White House
But discrimination, inequality, and injustice
Still exist
And attempts to disenfranchise people
Are on the rise
Fifty years later

America still struggles to write a better history
Fifty years later
Reminds us of a great event in American history
But fifty years later
Is yet another reminder
Of this country's dreadful past
And how so much has not changed in fifty years
Fifty years later is a time of commemoration
But it is also a time that we are reminded
Of the not so beautiful past of America
Fifty years ago
On the steps of the Lincoln Memorial
Many in America stood united, proud, and strong
Fifty years later
America must connect the road
From a half century ago
To the road of today
Completing this unfinished march
And fulfilling its dream
May the 50th anniversary
Of the March on Washington
Be deeper than historical reflections
May it be the blueprints
For the American dream for all
Let's truly let freedom ring
Fifty years later

64

I Love America

I love America
But sometimes America does not seem to love me
As I struggle to understand
How a nation would attack
The fundamental right to vote
Granted under our Constitution
A fundamental right
That wasn't always a fundamental right
My thoughts entertain an array of emotions
From anger to confusion to total disbelief
Because a price was paid
For all people to have the right to vote
Especially for African-Americans
And the battle for the right to vote to become law
Didn't come without its many challenges
People fought the long fight for the right to vote
And people died for the right to vote
And for five decades
The Voting Rights Act
Has protected the right to vote
For all Americans
But sadly
America is writing a new chapter in its history
A chapter of disgrace and embarrassment
A chapter that reveals America's current state
Of moral blindness
As I sit attempting to figure out the dynamics
Of this complicated democracy
As America uses words
Like nationalism and patriotism
I wonder if America truly understands
What those words mean
I love America
But sometimes America does not seem to love me

Because from 1965 to today
Everything has changed and nothing has changed
The precious right to vote is under attack
We have failed to remember the saying
That those who cannot remember the past
Are condemned to repeat it
And five decades later
The law that America had passed
To protect the right for all Americans to vote
Is in immediate jeopardy
The Supreme Court
The enforcer of America's Constitution
Has weakened parts of the Voting Rights Act
How can what has been a constitutional right
For five decades
No longer be a constitutional right?
If we believe in democracy
And for what America is supposed to stand for
Then we must believe in the right to vote
For all Americans
At the heart of the matter, is a matter of the heart
Because right is right and wrong is wrong
And this is wrong
Right now I am regretting America's past
And fearing America's future
Many states have changed laws
To require voter ID and other restrictions
To try to suppress voters' rights
They say these laws are designed
To prevent voter fraud
But there is virtually no evidence
That such fraud even exists
How can something be so wide spread
Yet so undetected?
All of this in the name of preventing
So-called voter fraud
America needs to wake up and smell the coffee
As we face continuing challenges
Of this new generation of voter suppression
Have memories fighting for voting rights faded?

I hope not!
Because the right to vote
Should be sacred in America
A price was paid for the right to vote
We must realize that the fight is far from over
We cannot depend on Congress, the president
Or the many states of this country
To protect the right to vote
Because they have proven they are not dependable
They have determined the facts to be irrelevant
I am tired of pretending to understand
The unexplainable
And even though sometimes America
Does not seem to love me
I love America

65

Brother to Brother

As iron sharpens iron
And as a bond can be stronger than steel
So should the brother to brother relationship be
Whether brothers by blood
Or connected by life's journey
The relationship and unity between brothers
Should always define and symbolize
What real brotherhood should be
Brotherhood is much deeper than the connection
Brotherhood is an allegiance
With meaning and purpose
Brotherhood is only as strong
As the commitment to the bond
And to the relationship that has developed
Brotherhood is an obligation
That demands accountability
Brotherhood is a feeling of knowing
A brother can believe in and count on
A fellow brother
Brotherhood is a difficult concept to define
Because when it is done right, it is extraordinary
Being in a true brother to brother relationship
Means you are your brother's keeper
And your brother is your keeper
Being in a true brother to brother relationship
Who you are will be transformed
Being in a true brother to brother relationship
You will become the man you were designed to be
Being in a true brother to brother relationship
Will help you to reach your full potential
And be the best that you can be
Being in a true brother to brother relationship
Will help you produce positive changes
In your character, convictions, and conduct

Being in a true brother to brother relationship
Will help in your commitment to do life God's way
When a brother to brother relationship is real
You will focus on doing what it takes
To maintain that relationship
Like eagles soar and lions roar
A brother to brother relationship
Reveals its strength
The true brother to brother relationship
Will reveal a bond that cannot be broken
Because a brother to brother relationship is strong
And it is never a source of abuse or neglect
As iron sharpens iron
And as a bond can be stronger than steel
So should the brother to brother relationship be
A brother to brother relationship does not mean
That those involved agree on every word
And every deed
But it is a brother to brother relationship
That challenges one to be a better person
It is a relationship that is open to correction
It is a relationship that helps one truly see himself
It is a relationship that helps those involved
Strengthen and develop the pursuit of God's heart
It is a relationship that will help those involved
Deal with the personal struggles of past regrets
It is a relationship that will help those involved
Deal with those partly cloudy
With a chance of thunderstorms type of days
A brother to brother relationship
Is a non-negotiable commitment
A brother to brother relationship
Is an uncompromising commitment
A brother to brother relationship
Is a support system commitment
A brother to brother relationship
Is an encouragement commitment
A brother to brother relationship
Is a relationship that edifies
A brother to brother relationship

Has photographic, yet short term memory
A brother to brother relationship
Is a relationship that learns from the past
So the future can be all that it can be
A brother to brother relationship
Encourages the pursuit of dreams
No obstacle can block the path
Of brothers united for life
As iron sharpens iron
And as a bond can be stronger than steel
So should the brother to brother relationship be

66

I Wish I Could Have Just One More Day

I had convinced myself what always was
Would always be
Too often taking for granted
The blessings and gifts of life
And living life as if those we love
Would physically be around forever
But sadly, many of the people we love dearly
Will leave our lives
And what we thought would be forever
Turns out to be a loved one
Whose life journey has come to an end
A life that has been taken away
Long before we were ready for it to leave
A life that will no longer travel with ours
Becomes a painful reminder
That this is just the way life works
And that this is just a part of our life's journey
From the moment we enter this world
We are being introduced to people
And we are saying goodbye to people
But I too often struggle with saying goodbye
And though I know my loved ones
Are in a better place
I often wish that they were still here with me
For just one more day
I know the loss of a loved one
Is something we all have to deal with
But it still hurts when the voice is gone
I know when someone is in your heart
They are never gone
But something is still missing
You can no longer say all that was in your heart
If I could just have one more conversation

One more chance to make up for the time
That I thought would be here forever
All of the times that I took for granted
Now I wish I could see my loved ones again
But in this earthly life it will never be
Never again will I
Hear the voice of my loved ones
Or hear their laugher
Or share those great stories
Or hug and kiss my loved ones
Or enjoy one more home-cooked meal
Or receive the advice and life lessons
Or make new memories
And never again will I have just be able to say
"I love you."
I wish I could just have one more day
Maybe I would give my best attempt to share
All that is living in my heart
Maybe I would talk
Until I could not say another word
Maybe I would just, "I love you."
Or maybe, "I miss you."
If I had one more day
I would put a footprint in my mind
So that I would never forget that day
I would try to share all of the words
That I'd like to say
Words that are held captive in my heart
I would give anything for just one more day
To see the faces, the smiles, to hear the voices
And to feel once again
The presence of the amazing love of those I loved
Beyond the fears
Beyond the tears
Beyond the ache
In a heart broken from the loss of loved ones
I know there is a place of peace
And though my heart may feel abandoned
I am never alone
The beautiful memories with my loved ones

Are in my heart forever
And as new day after new day arrives
Without the presence of those who are gone
I still know that my loved ones are with me
In my heart and in my mind
And with that belief comes a peace
An assurance that we will always be together
And in that peace
I promise there will be no tomorrows
Void of me taking the time to talk to my loved ones
I can still hear their voices
I can still see their faces
And I know exactly what they would say to me
Because of the love that made them my loved ones
And if I had one more day - and I truly wish I did
I would sing out words like never before
I would not take for granted
What could be our last day
I wish I could have just one more day

67

The Power of Prayer

Mama didn't always understand
Why things happened
But Mama always believed that God was in control
Mama prayed for those she knew
Mama prayed for those she didn't know
She believed prayer could change lives
She believed prayer could transform the world
She believed there was power in prayer
Mama prayed because that was who she was
A praying mother, wife, woman
And a committed follower of God
Mama believed in fervent and persistent prayer
Mama prayed earnestly, regularly
And passionately
Mama prayed many times a day
Mama understood prayer's place in her life
She never found it difficult
To go to the Lord in prayer
God did not always answer her prayers
When and how she thought He would
But He always answered her prayers
God's answered prayers always touched her heart
And increased her faith in God
And her strength came from her faith in God
Mama believed in the power of prayer
Mama didn't just pray for herself
But Mama believed in praying for others
Through her joys and pain
Mama prayed
Through her own struggles and health problems
Mama prayed
Through her successes and trials of parenting
Mama prayed
Through the challenges of a broken marriage

Mama prayed
Through the sickness and death of loved ones
Mama prayed
Mama prayed because that is what she knew
Mama didn't only pray for those she loved
Mama prayed for everyone
Mama prayed for family problems
Health problems
Financial problems
World problems
Mama believed that prayer was the catalyst
To solving the problems in the world
Mama prayed for the neglected, poor and sick
Mama prayed about the crime, corruption
And violence
Mama prayed about the killings, murders
And tragedies
Mama prayed for the local, national
And world leaders
Mama truly believed in the power of prayer
Mama's prayers had a deep and lasting influence
In the lives of her children
If it was not for Mama's prayers
I don't know where my life would have taken me
Mama's prayers helped to guide and protect me
In a world that could have easily destroyed me
Mama's prayers taught me how to pray
Mama's prayers taught me how to put God first
And to put my trust in Him
Mama's prayers gave me lessons about life
That life could have never given
Mama's prayers were filled with love
Mama's prayers taught me the importance
Of caring and praying for others
And for what was going on in the world around me
Mama's prayers developed and molded me
Into the man that I have become
My heart to help and pray for those in need
Is a result of a praying mother
My passion for writing

Is a result of a praying mother
Addressing injustice, issues and world problems
Through prose is because of my praying mother
Mama believed in the power of prayer
Her faithful prayer sessions with God
Became lessons for me and those she loved
God showed Mama who He wanted her to be
And who He designed her to be
And she, being a faithful praying woman
Made a great impact on the lives of those she loved
Especially in the life of her son
To put it simply
Mama believed in the power of prayer

68

Our Children Are Dying

Now I lay me down to sleep,
I pray the Lord my soul to keep,
May angels watch me through the night
And keep me safe till morning's light

Our children should not have to fear
If they will see the morning's light
Our children should not have to fear
What a new day can bring or take away
Our children should not have to feel
As if they are living in a war zone
But for many of our children
This is what life has become
Unfortunately in our society
Many of our children are living in fear
And sadly, many of our children are dying
Hearts are broken daily
As the loved ones of young victims
Of senseless violence mourn over their loss
As we struggle with more and more birthdays
Graduations and special moments being stolen
We have to also deal with the fact
That there will be no new memories made
We have become a society full of the daily news
Reporting the tragedies of young people dying
As if they are reporting the evening sports scores
So many children are dying
And so many parents are crying
Yet we still are not treating violence in America
As if it is a national crisis
We have become a society where yellow tape
And the closing of caskets
Have become reminders
Of the darkness of our reality

We have become a society
Where our children pray about
Their fear that tomorrow
May be their last tomorrow
Rather than prayers of the brightness
Of their futures
We have become a society where our parents pray
About their children just returning safely home
From school or from the playground
The death of young people to gun violence
Has become as American as baseball and apple pie
We are constantly reminded
That young people dying is now symbolic
Of the violent culture of America
A culture of violence that has become a life of fear
For many Americans
Inner-city blues have invited the inner-city fears
Fears that walking to school
Or sitting in front of your house can be deadly
Fears that walking down the street to the park
Or walking to the playground can be deadly
Fears that a random act of violence
Could quickly steal the dreams
Of a promising future
Fears of one young life being stolen
Before another life truly begins
Fears that are so very real for many in America
Wake up America!
When did we stop caring about life?
Especially the lives of our children
How can a young lady perform
At the inaugural events
For the President of the United States one week
And two weeks later become another victim
Of gun violence in America
And yet there is still no call for a national debate
To combat this crisis in America
As we sit and wait for the next high profile killing
America should be getting tired
Tired because the violence continues to be ignored

In a country where it is more important
To protect the rights of gun owners
Than it is to protect innocent lives
How do we deal with so many fears?
How do we deal with so many tears?
How do we deal with trying to explain
The death of classmate or friend?
How do we deal with trying to explain to a child
The insanity that is destroying a society?
Must we all lose a loved one to violence
Before we realize the seriousness of this crisis?
We should be sick and tired of hearing
About one tragedy after another
When will this epidemic
Of our children dying to gun violence
Become a national priority?
We cannot become comfortable
With our children dying
We must not become so accepting of gun violence
Becoming embedded in our society
We can no longer allow our children's lives
To be stolen without an effort to protect them
It takes a village to raise a child
And it takes a village to protect a child
We can no longer be a contributor to this betrayal
Of the American dream
Our children are a gift from God
And He expects us to protect them
So let's take away the fears
And allow every child to enjoy the blessings
That a new day may bring

Now I lay me down to sleep
I pray the Lord my soul to keep
May angels watch me through the night
And keep me safe till morning's light

Amen!

69

Two Hundred Seventy-Six

Two hundred seventy-six
Is much more than just a number
Two hundred seventy-six
Is much more than a total amount
Two hundred seventy-six
Is much more than an answer to an equation
Two hundred seventy-six
Is a reminder that lives were stolen
Two hundred seventy-six
Is a reminder of a crime against humanity
Two hundred seventy-six
Is a reminder of the girls who were kidnapped
Two hundred seventy-six
Is a reminder of the girls who were missing
Two hundred seventy-six
Should keep us from forgetting about the girls
Who were only seeking an education
But instead were abducted
In a horrible and senseless act of terror
Two hundred seventy-six
Is a number that should remind the world
That a nightmare that existed
For two hundred seventy-six girls
And their families
Two hundred seventy-six
Is much more than just a number
Two hundred seventy-six
Is a number that should be on our hearts
On our minds and in our prayers
It does not matter
If these girls were Christian, Muslim
Or any other religion
What matters
Is that two hundred seventy-six girls weren't home

Where they belonged
And because of that fact
There should have been a crisis
And a state of emergency
The United Nations
And its inconsistent counterfeit world policies
On human rights and crimes against humanity
Has once again failed
As the world failed to react in all deliberate speed
These two hundred seventy-six girls were missing
Each day passed with another dream unfulfilled
And with the return of the nightmare
That just wouldn't go away
As America retreated from saving lives
And picked and chose what deserves its attention
Two hundred seventy-six girls were still missing
And their lives were in serious danger
Two hundred seventy-six girls were living
In constant fear of death, physical abuse
Rape and the threat of being sold into slavery
But did their lives matter at all
Or were they just insignificant pawns
In a game of political chess?
When an Afghanistan girl was shot by the Taliban
For attending school
She became an international hero
And received worldwide media attention
When two hundred seventy-six Nigerian girls
Were attacked and kidnapped for attending school
What we had was a delayed reaction
For weeks the story was barely mentioned
The silence revealed the importance of the lives
Of the two hundred seventy-six girls
There was not even an Amber alert
But months and millions of dollars were spent
Looking for a missing Malaysian plane
That crashed
But we didn't seem to care
About two hundred seventy-six missing girls
Who were alive and taken by a terrorist group

America has been quick to respond
Regarding issues in the Middle East
And in the Ukraine
But Africa seemed to be neglected and ignored
When will the eyes of the blind open
Because two hundred seventy-six
Should be much more than just a number
Enough about the rehashing of Benghazi
Not that it wasn't a tragedy
But two hundred seventy-six lives
Were more important
Because if you don't know
Terrorist hideaways have become the new homes
For two hundred seventy-six girls who were stolen
"Bring Back Our Girls"
Should have been more than a campaign
Of international awareness
Those abducted schoolgirls were our daughters
Sisters and friends
Two hundred seventy-six
Is much more than three digits of insignificance
Two hundred seventy-six
Is a number we should not ignore
The world should have stood together
Against this crime against humanity
To take those girls back to their families
We have a moral obligation to respond
And to take any necessary action
Because life matters
The abductors said western education is sinful
But what was sinful
Were the senseless attacks
On these innocent children
Two hundred seventy-six
Was much more than just a number
It was a call for the world to bring home
Two hundred seventy-six girls

Words Are Powerful

To me words are powerful
Words are the evidence of the strength
Of self-expression
Words reveal what needs to be said
Often exactly when it needs to be said
Without words, we all live in silence
When silence needs to be broken
Words are the sound of the trumpet
That transforms nothing into something
Words have the power
To transform a wrong into a right
Words have the power
To change a bad situation into a good situation
Words often free us from the bondage
Of what life sometimes brings
Words are like precious jewels in a treasure box
That when used properly
Reveal a beauty that cannot be denied
It is often said, "Actions speak louder than words."
But the right words at the right moment
Can speak just as loudly
To me words are more than just words
To me words are powerful
Words search the chambers of our hearts
And tell the stories of who we are
Words are the expressions that defend, define
And describe who we are
Words reveal our life experiences
On this journey that have made us who we are
To me words are more than just words
Words are the tools used to turn dreams
Into realities
Words are the combinations of sounds
That express something meaningful

Words are a covenant, oath, promise, or vow
Words are a command, a directive, or an order
Words are a comment, quote, or response
Words are alliterations, similes
And striking metaphors
Words are more than something that sounds deep
Because the words we use
Reveal who we truly are
Words are powerful
Words stimulate our thoughts and open our minds
Words reveal the truth that resides in our heart
Words reveal love
Words reveal passion
Words reveal respect
Words reveal wisdom
Words are often very simple, yet very complex
Words are so deep they penetrate the heart
And place a footprint on the mind
Words, when used correctly, communicate truths
Truths that are fully accepted, embraced
And never forgotten
Words have no boundaries
Words allow us fly further and soar higher
Words help us grow and reach our full potential
Words are the poems and stories
That touch our lives
Words are "I Have a Dream" and "I Will Rise"
Words express the inspiration and motivation
That made us who we are
To me words are powerful

Acts of Love?

Behind a wall of silence
Lies the depth of what was thought to be
Acts of love
Hidden tears conceal what was not meant
To be seen
How the abnormal becomes the normal
How the unacceptable becomes the acceptable
How the acts of love
Become unspoken expressions of love
A life once full of dreams
Becomes a life full of brokenness
Broken dreams
Broken hearts
Broken promises
Broken love
Acts of love
Become confusion and contradiction of love
Acts of love
Become the abuse and violence
That do not resemble true love
Acts of love
Create a false belief of what is the new normal
But in reality, it is anything but normal
Memories consist of what we wish
Had never happened
For far too many women
The silent screams are too often not heard
Victims' realities are unknown
To those around them
It seems as if their lives do not matter
But their lives do matter
Wives matter
Mothers matter
Daughters matter
Sisters matter

All women matter
This damaged act of love is well hidden from many
Countless women live their lives
Behind a mask of deception
Countless women trick the world into believing
That their lives are normal
Countless women convince others
That they are truly happy
Disguised as love, abuse is abuse
And abuse is never acceptable
Abuse says to children
That it is okay to beat a woman
Abuse says to young girls
That it is okay to be beaten in an act of love
Abuse says to young men
That it is okay to physically assault a woman
Cycles of abuse send so many false messages
Of what true love is
These acts of abuse and violence
Disguise themselves as acts of love
These acts of abuse and violence
Destroy marriages, families, and lives
These acts of abuse
Create fake smiles and false images
Of happiness and joy
A history of abuse and violence
Does not have to be a future of abuse and violence
Shattered reflections of a marred picture of love
Can be restored
We must end the inner hurt and pain
Caused by so-called "acts of love"
We must honor, love, and protect our women
We must respect, strengthen
And support our women
We must create a path for healing
We must restore what "acts of love" have stolen
These acts of love are never acceptable
Domestic abuse of women must stop
So that acts of love can return to truly being
Acts of love

A Moment

Sometimes life offers us something
We have never experienced before
Sometimes a story begins, a chapter is created
Or a memory is made
Sometimes life offers us a gift
That we will always cherish and never forget
Sometimes life will offer us something very simple
Yet so profound
Sometimes life will offer us a special moment
A moment that often appears in our lives
Just when it is needed
A moment that often comes
As an unexpected fulfillment of what
Has been living in our heart
A moment that has such an impact on our lives
That it becomes a part of who we are
A moment so distinct
That it helps to define who we have become
A moment so perfect, that even in its brevity
It transforms into something
That will last a lifetime
A moment so pure that it cannot hide the reality
That reveals the true us
Sometimes life offers us a moment
That will truly change our existence
A moment, that when pondered
Remains in our mind forever
But the reality is, the moment is brief
A brief moment that helps us realize
That dreams were more than just dreams
And that dreams really can come true
A moment is special

Because it seems to have perfect timing
A moment has a way of living
In our hearts and minds
A moment has a way of running through thoughts
Over and over again
Like a classic movie rerun
A moment has a way of connecting our past
Our present and our future
A moment can be truly special
A moment can be as special
As an amazing love story
A moment can be as special
As a gathering with friends
A moment can be as special
As a reunion with family
A moment can be as special
As witnessing history being made
A moment is more than a life experience
Stored in a memory box
A moment is a valued time
From a chapter in life that is so precious
That you and your life can be forever changed
In a moment

73

Identity Crisis

When I looked in the mirror
I failed to recognize the reflection
The person I thought I knew
I no longer recognized
Everything I was and everything I thought I knew
Were no longer familiar
The memory of who I was
And the mystery of who I had become
Created a feeling of confusion and a sense of loss
An identity crisis conflicted my view of myself
I had a feeling that something was different
I had a feeling that something was missing
I had a feeling that the person I was
Had been replaced
I had a feeling that I had lost myself
Along this journey through life
All that life offered stole my life away
Without me even realizing it
The life I spent my lifetime planning
Didn't prepare me for this internal crisis
An identity crisis
An identity crisis has occurred
Without me realizing it
I evolved into someone I hardly know
I never thought my dreams, goals
And life experiences would transform me
Transform me into someone who fooled everyone
Transforming me into someone who fooled me
I never thought I would become lost in my efforts
To be the best that I could be
Doing all of the right things
My life became a personal commitment

To family, church, and work
A personal commitment
To whatever life brought my way
My life made me invisible to myself
And through what I thought was transparency
I was still unable to see that I lost me to myself
At some point along my journey
I forgot about myself
I forgot about what made me who I thought I was
Dreams were fulfilled, but something was lost
Goals were achieved, but something was missing
Life was good
But I no longer recognized the man in the mirror
The intimate connection of knowing
And understanding myself was broken
I always thought I knew who I was
I always thought I knew my strengths
I always thought I knew my weaknesses
I always thought I knew what I loved
I always thought I knew what I did not like
I always thought I knew what was in my heart
I always thought I knew what I stood for
But at some point, I seemed to have lost
Some of what I thought I knew about myself
I had always been able to confess my failures
Shortcomings and sins
I had always been able to look at my life
And tell when something was wrong
But I guess when everything in life was working
Except me, it was easy to forget about me
Those things that made me the person that I was
Are now ignored
And those things that over the years
Had become the necessary needs
That kept my life in order and in a perfect rhythm
Are now lost
My identity crisis was real and I was losing myself

The obligations and responsibilities of life
Have changed me into a programmed droid
I have become totally committed to everyone
And everything assigned to me
But somewhere along this journey
I forgot about myself
Life had presented me with many lessons
But somewhere I missed the lesson
On me remembering to take care of me
So today when I look in the mirror
I will smile proudly at the man
Who tried his best to be the man
He was designed to be
But I will also look into the eyes of that man
And say, "I am sorry for neglecting you for so long
And from now on I promise to make sure
That all of your needs are met
And make time to do those things
That have made you the person you are."
A broken man who has lost himself
Can only be so good to himself
And to those he loves
So on this day, my journey starts
With rediscovering me
If you look in the mirror who would you see?
A person in perfect harmony with life
Or a person with an identity crisis?

74

God Made You Very Special and Very Special You Are

A Poem for My Four Children

When God made you He made you very special
And very special you are
The design God gave you
He did not give to anyone else
Your design was perfectly thought out just for you
From the shade of your brown skin
To the number of hairs on your head
It was all a part of God's perfect design
God gave you what He wanted you to have
When God breathed life into you
It was not just to create a life
God's desire was for you to live a life of purpose
And a life of meaning
God's desire was for you to live a life for Him
God made you very special
And very special you are
God loves you so much
That He gave you two parents
Who love you more than you could ever know
God loves you so much
That He gave you two parents
To protect, teach, and raise you for Him
God loves you so much that He gave you siblings
With a love for you that is so strong
That it will be there for you always
God made you special
And very special you are

God loves you so much
That He thought of you when He sent His Son
Jesus to die for your sins
And to reconcile you back to Him
God has loved you from the day He created you
God made you unique
God made you very special
And very special you are
God gave you a heart to feel
And to know when others are in need
God gave you the ability to love and to receive love
God gave you a smile that could make others smile
God gave you the strength
To lift others up when they are down
God made you very special
And very special you are
God gave you intelligence and a brain capacity
That will allow you to learn anything
God gave you the abilities
To do amazing and incredible things
God created you to be a light to the world
God created you for the purpose of serving Him
And bringing lives to Him
God created you to be all that you can be for Him
God created you to reach your full potential
God created you to succeed
God created you to do everything to glorify Him
God made you very special
And very special you are
In seven days God had created the world
And everything in it
And when He was done, it was good!
When God created you and looked over His work
And saw how amazing and gifted you were
He said, "You are good!"
Because God made you very special
And very special you are

Reflection

If you look into a mirror
Would you recognize the reflection you would see?
Would the reflection resemble you
Or would it be a stranger looking back at you?
Would the reflection reveal the authentic you
Or would it reveal a false image of you?
Would the reflection in a mirror
Reveal who you really are?
Would the reflection in a mirror
Reveal your strengths and weaknesses?
Would the reflection in a mirror
Reveal the best and the worst of you?
If you look into the eyes of the reflection
Would those eyes allow you to see yourself?
Would a look into the eyes of the reflection
Allow you to see your heart, mind, and soul?
Would a look into the eyes of the reflection
Allow a transparency that would reveal
Who you truly are?
Would a look into the eyes of the reflection
Reveal someone with strength beyond measure?
Would a look into a mirror
Reflect bravery, confidence and courage?
Would a look into a mirror
Reflect honesty, truth and integrity?
Would a look into a mirror
Reflect an image that does not compromise
Who you proclaim to be and who you want to be?
Would a look into a mirror
Reflect your love for self, others, and life?
When you look into a mirror
Who do you see looking back at you?

Would you be blind to what the reflection presents
Or would you recognize and acknowledge the truth
Of what the reflection reveals?
The reflection in the mirror
Is more than just a bounce-back image of you
The reflection in the mirror
Is a moment of self-reflection
The reflection in the mirror
Is an opportunity for a personal self-inventory
An opportunity to look at the life
That is being lived and is reflected back
A look in a mirror
Can make the unknown known
And the unconscious conscious
A look in the mirror
Can confront inadequacies, failures, and mistakes
A look in the mirror
Can deal with the poor decisions
That have been made
A look in the mirror
Can help you discover your true reflection
A look in the mirror
Can unlock the fullness of your life
A look in the mirror
Can create a vision for a better tomorrow
Too often we fail to see the true reflection
When we look into a mirror
A look into the mirror
Is the opportunity to look at your past
Examine your present and to see your future
If you look into a mirror
Would you recognize the reflection?
Would the reflection resemble you
Or would it be a stranger looking back at you?

I Am Unapologetically Me

I am who I am and I am who I was created to be
And though society has continuously attempted
To falsely define and inaccurately describe me
I do know who I am and who I was designed to be
From America's beginning until now
I have been misperceived, misrepresented
And misunderstood
The efforts to dehumanize me
And make me less than a human being
Have failed in their attempts to create false truths
From the slave auction posters advertising slavery
To the constant negative attacks
On America's first black President
America has attempted to falsely define me
America has a long history
Of attempting to make me
Into someone that I am not
But I know who I am
And I know who I was created to be
Inaccuracies and false illusions
Have perpetuated a misunderstanding of who I am
False images have created false messages
That influence attitudes, ideas
And opinions about me
Brainwashing has created
Negative mental pictures
Of who I am supposed to be
And continues to keep America
Confused and divided
The misrepresentation of me
Created the myth of my inferiority
The misrepresentation of me

Created my mental, physical
And psychological enslavement
The misrepresentation of me
Affected the many generations
That came before me
The misrepresentation of me
Justified so much ugliness
Of some of America's not so beautiful past
The misrepresentation of me
Allowed negative labels and perceptions
To create a false illusion of me
But I refuse to accept the poor portrayals
That perpetuate negative stereotypes of me
I am who I am and I am who I was created to be
I am not an abusive husband
I am not a missing father
I am not a violent threat to a world
I am not a drug-dealing criminal
I am not a thug or menace to society
I am not the negative image
That the big screen has made me out to be
I know me
I believe in me
I understand me
I am who I am and I am who I was created to be
I am unapologetically me

What Does Your Tomorrow Look Like?

What if you could look into the future
And see what your tomorrows would be like?
Would you be able to handle
What the future would bring?
Would tomorrow be welcomed with open arms?
Or would there be a fear to open the door
To what tomorrow would reveal?
Would tomorrow bring the beauty
That a new day is supposed to bring?
Or would tomorrow come with an unexpected
Surprise or resemble a bad dream?
Would tomorrow be the fulfillment
Of what you hope every new day would be?
The hope that would usher in
A day of new opportunities
A tomorrow that would be another step
Up the ladder of a bright future
What does your tomorrow look like?
Would tomorrow be different from today
Yesterday, and the day before?
Would tomorrow be a good day
Or would it be a bad day?
Would tomorrow be the continuation
Of an upward climb
Or would it be a downward spiral?
If life is going well
Would tomorrow follow suit
And continue the good life?
If life has been not so good
Would tomorrow be like walking through a door
That will bring a re-occurrence of bad choices
Past mistakes and poor decisions?

Would tomorrow be that defining moment
At the crossroads of life
That could change your life's direction?
What does your tomorrow look like?
Would tomorrow reveal goals being met
And plans for life being achieved?
Would tomorrow be another building block
Defining a proud legacy?
What does your tomorrow look like?
Would tomorrow be a day to remember?
Or would tomorrow be a day
That would be best forgotten?
We cannot make tomorrows
What we want them to be
But what we do today
Can help make tomorrow a good day
Tomorrows should be beautiful
Tomorrows should bring joy
Tomorrows should always be special
So what does your tomorrow look like?

I Love Lincoln University

From the moment I stepped on campus
I knew I was where I was supposed be
I loved the beautiful campus
That seemed to be in the middle of nowhere
I loved the many people
Who came from all over the world
With dreams and stories just like mine
I loved the rich and high quality education offered
And the tradition
That made Lincoln University very special
I loved the history, heritage, and legacy
That made the Lincoln University experience
Truly unique
The Lincoln University experience
Was like no other experience
The Lincoln University experience
Taught me the secret to success in life
The Lincoln University experience
Painted a clear picture of the obligations
That were required to represent the university
The Lincoln University experience
Was my climb towards defining my future
And my pilgrimage to becoming
Who I was meant to be
I love Lincoln University
Because Lincoln University became a part of me
Lincoln University transcended academics
And helped me to see my American dream
A dream that reminded me of the real truth
That my life mattered
A dream that taught me to live life without limits
A dream that taught me

To not throw away my tomorrows
And to protect my future
Lincoln University taught me
To take my dreams to a new plateau
Lincoln University taught me
How to turn my dreams into reality
I love Lincoln University
Because love is a way of life there
Lincoln University is where
Everyone seemed to know everyone
Lincoln University is where
Everyone seemed to have a love for each other
Lincoln University is where
Love is a reflection of its identity
An identity that defines a legacy that lives in me
A legacy of developing great minds
A legacy of producing great leaders
A legacy of alumni
Who have distinguished themselves
As doctors, lawyers, educators, business people
Theologians and heads of state
A legacy of many distinctions
I am a living legacy of Lincoln University
Over 160 years have passed
Since Lincoln University opened its doors
Yet it is still relevant today
Lincoln University is deeply rooted in our past
And it still manages to shape the future
Lincoln University will never become irrelevant
Because there will always be a need
For what Lincoln University has to offer
Lincoln University helped me to confront my fears
Lincoln University helped me to see myself
Who I was and who I was to become
Lincoln University gave me confidence
Lincoln University gave me strength
Lincoln University taught me many lessons

**Lincoln University prepared me for the real world
Lincoln University helped me reach
My full potential
Before there was a commencement
Lincoln University prepared me for life
Before I received a degree
Lincoln University challenged, inspired
And motivated me
To make a difference in the world
Before I was an alumni
Lincoln University taught me to proudly represent
The Orange and Blue
I love Lincoln University
I love the institution, whose principal mission was
And is to develop, educate, and train
People like me
I love Lincoln University
I will always owe this great institution
A debt of gratitude
And because Lincoln University loved me
I love Lincoln University**

Love Tells a Story

From love's beginning and after each new chapter
Love reveals how special love is
From an initial encounter
To the making of memories
Love tells a story that only love could create
As one heart opens to another
An intimate connection is born
That becomes a story of real love
A story that is the fulfillment of many dreams
A story of a dream that has found the door
To its reality
A dream that reveals that love is real
And that a love story can come true
A story that brings out the newness of love
A story that details the depths of love
A story that paints a picture
Of the intimacies of love
A story that reveals the strength of love
Love tells a story
An introduction that turns into a friendship
A friendship that turns into a relationship
A relationship that turns into a romance
A romance that turns into two souls becoming one
And soulmates becoming a deep love story
Love tells a story
As the mind entertains emotions felt by the heart
And discovers all of the priceless treasures
Residing in the heart
The beauty of what love has become is formed
And becomes the expression
Of what love was meant to be
Acts of love telling a story

Of two hearts beating as one
And new chapter after new chapter
Sharing the power of what love has become
Love always tell a story
A story that is based on emotions and feelings
That are constantly growing
A story that brings new experiences
Like the beginning of new days
A story that seems to have a feel of perfection
As two hearts open up to each other
A story that is enhanced by each new experience
That love brings
Love tells a story
A story filled with adventure, excitement
And spontaneous moments
That make love so amazing and every day special
A story that patiently awaits the next chapter
For the creation of what will become
Another precious memory
A story that tells of the significance
Of the existence of a love that is limitless
And unconditional
Love tells a story that is far from being perfect
But often feels perfect
From love's beginning and after each new chapter
Love tells a story

I Love Reading

I do not know if reading discovered me
Or if I discovered reading
But what I do know is that at a very early age
A very intimate relationship was born
My parents inspired the relationship
My sisters encouraged the relationship
My teachers helped me grow in the relationship
And what started out as an introduction to books
Became a part of me
I love reading
And I have always loved my reading relationship
They say that reading is fundamental
And I truly believe that reading helped build
The foundation of who I am
Reading became the origin
Of my new life discoveries
Reading helped me to absorb everything
That life had to offer
Reading developed my mind
In ways that I never imagined
Reading kidnapped my mind
And helped me better understand
This journey called life
For me, reading has always been like listening
Reading helped me understand the misunderstood
Reading allowed me to see anywhere in the world
Without needing to travel
Reading allowed me to meet many amazing people
Without a formal introduction
Reading allowed me to visit the past
And to see the future
Reading transformed written words

Into pictures in my mind
Reading produced what has become a long
Intimate relationship with words
Reading allowed me to see the creativity
That existed within me
Reading took me on one adventure after another
Connecting my imagination to my dreams
Reading taught me about me
Reading was my teacher, my tutor, my friend
Reading took my mind on a journey
That expanded my comprehension and intellect
Reading increased my ability to do anything
My confidence to try anything
And my determination to achieve anything
Reading revealed my strengths and weaknesses
Reading armed and prepared me
For all that life could throw at me
Reading became the building blocks of my life
Reading educated me on my many life interests
Reading guided me on the path
That became my destiny
Reading helped me to fall in love with words
Reading books brought me joy
Reading poetry taught me the art of expression
Reading stories took me on personal journeys
Reading became my addiction
Reading spoke to my heart, spirit, and soul
Reading developed and molded me
In ways that I would have never imagined
Reading helped me understand myself
Reading helped me connect with others
Reading helped me understand others
Reading helped me understand
What my eyes did not always see
Reading taught me life lessons
And taught me about my profound history
Reading assembled the broken pieces

Of my ancestor's diaspora
That helped define who I am
Reading helped me understand
That I was different and unique
Reading helped me understand
That I was strong and very special
Understanding the written word
Has deeply helped me understand myself
Since the time I was introduced to reading
I love reading

Three Shelves

I would not be who I am
If not for my love for books
My love for reading introduced me to everything
My mind thirsts for
And it was that thirst that led me to bookstores
My visits to bookstores
Were always able to quench my thirst
The availability for whatever my mind desired
Seemed endless
And the many shelves of books
Fed my mind like the food that nourished my body
My visits to the bookstores
Took me on many adventures
And formally introduced me to many people
The shelves of books introduced me to the writings
Of Phillis Wheatley, Paul Laurence Dunbar
Zora Neale Hurston and many others
The shelves of books made me feel
Like I was experiencing the Harlem Renaissance
The shelves of books gave me
Go Tell It on the Mountain, Invisible Man
Native Son, Roots, A Raisin in the Sun
The Color Purple, The Souls of Black Folks
The shelves of books taught me about
The ongoing fight for equality, freedom and justice
But most of all the shelves of books
Helped me discover me
There were always shelves of books
That I identified with as an African American
Growing up in a world full of discrimination
Double standards and racism
A world that did not always recognize or respect

The journey of a people
Who helped to build America
The shelves of books
Helped me transcend my reality
The shelves of books
Helped me to understand me
The many shelves of books
Introduced me to my past
The many shelves of books
Taught me to be confident
The many shelves of books
Taught me to be proud
The many shelves of books
Taught me to hope and dream
The many shelves of books
Painted a picture of my future
But I would have never thought my sanctuary
For knowledge in bookstores
Would turn into just three shelves of books
On a hidden bookcase
I would have never thought the shelves of books
That gave me the ability to dream
Would disappear
I would have never thought the shelves of books
That helped me to discover me
Would be relegated to just three shelves
Three shelves of books reveal the new reality
That books about and by African Americans
Are no longer relevant
Three shelves of books reveal how books
That present the experience and journey
Of African Americans
From an African American point of view
Are in a state of silent crisis
Three shelves of books reveal
That the rich history and legacy
Of the African American Experience

Is no longer worth promoting or selling
Three shelves of books reveal there is no longer
A need to provide shelves of books
That provide educational lessons
And positive self-images
To a people whose legacy has been stolen
Three shelves of books reveal
That books about African Americans
Are endangered
And may soon be missing all together
Three shelves of books reveal
What has become a literary tragedy
And a new reality

82

A Broken Democracy

Only a broken democracy would attempt
To redefine what true democracy means
In America
Only a broken democracy would allow
A vacant Supreme Court Justice seat
To remain vacant for a year
While attempts were being made to win
A political battle over the White House
Only a broken democracy would attempt
To block the President of the United States
From doing what he was elected, obligated
And required to do
Only a broken democracy would allow
Obstructionism to prevail
And become an adopted and attempted policy
To divide and dishonor a nation
Only a broken form of democracy would paint
A picture of a constitutional crisis
In an America where the interpretation of the law
Has become beyond comprehension
America and its democracy is broken
A broken democracy
That reveals America's deep divide
A divide between Democrats and Republicans
A divide between conservatives, moderates
And liberals
A divide caused by a lack of respect
For culture, race, and religion
A divide that is deeper than the nomination
Of a potential Supreme Court Justice
By the president of this country

A divide that caused many members
Of the Senate to vow
To never accept or confirm a recommendation
To America's highest court
Democracy is broken in America
And the death of a Supreme Court Justice
Is showing the world how broken democracy
In America really is
Only a broken democracy would challenge a sitting
President's ability to do the right thing
Before his actions reveal what he is doing is wrong
Only a broken democracy would rather shut
The government down
Than allow the government to function
As it is designed to operate
Only a broken democracy would lack the discipline
Honor and integrity to do what needs to be done
When it needs to be done
Despite the political games
No matter how strong the efforts may be
A wrong cannot be turned into a right
It is unethical and there is no precedent
For America to ignore the constitutional process
In filling a vacant seat on the Supreme Court
We, the people of the United States of America
Are a broken picture of a more perfect union
We are more of an example of a divided nation
We have failed to establish justice
And to insure domestic tranquility
We have lost sight of what it takes
To promote general welfare
And to secure the blessings of liberty
And posterity for all Americans
We, the people of the United States of America
Have become a broken democracy

83

To God Be the Glory

Fifty years of marriage
Is called the golden anniversary
It is a special time to celebrate the bond
That marks a half-century of togetherness
Commitment and strength
Fifty years of marriage
Is not only a celebration of longevity
But it is a blessing for all to see
Fifty years
Reveal what can happen when you put God first
Fifty years
Reveal what marriage looks like
When it resembles God's design
Fifty years
Reveal what happens in a God-centered marriage
Fifty years of marriage and to God be the glory
Because after fifty years
What God has put together has stayed together
Fifty years ago a covenant with God was made
Symbolizing two people coming together
And becoming a special union
Fifty years ago a commitment was made
To honor serve and worship God
In his perfect design for marriage
Fifty years ago a dream to build a future together
Became a reality
The exchanging of two rings symbolized
A heart-to-heart connection
The vows spoken promised a commitment
To each other and to God

Fifty years ago
Began the showering of many blessings
That revealed the amazing and unconditional love
Of our Heavenly Father
And now after fifty years of living a life together
To God we must give all of the glory and honor
For what He has done, is doing and will do
A half-century ago something wonderful began
And now we call it golden
Marriage in its purest form is precious
And shines like gold
And fifty years of marriage in its rarity
Is truly special and it is golden
A golden anniversary symbolizes the embracing
Of God's design for marriage
A golden anniversary symbolizes
A marriage with a foundation
Built through a strong faith in Jesus Christ
A golden anniversary symbolizes the compromises
Sacrifices and unselfish acts
That are needed to make a marriage golden
A golden anniversary is a reflection
Of both the good times and bad times
Because fifty years of marriage
Comes with some challenges
A golden anniversary symbolizes
The presence of God in the lives of two people
Who understand they could not have done it alone
A half-century of a continuing legacy
And precious memories
And to God be the Glory
So many stories can be shared
From this union of 50 years
So many lessons can be taught
From two hearts becoming one
And choosing to practice marriage
The way God designed it

God has given the gift of a lifetime friend, partner
Encourager, and supporter
For fifty years God has shown His commitment
For fifty years God has shown His devotion
For fifty years God has shown His love
And after fifty years
God's gift has become a picture
Of what love truly is
And to God be the glory

84

A Mother's Love

God knew exactly what we needed
When He created mothers
He knew we would need to be nurtured
Raised and taught
He knew we would need direction and guidance
He knew we would need a nurse
He knew we would need a counselor
To give advice and teach life lessons
He knew we would need someone
To wipe away our tears in times of pain
He knew we would need a mother's love
A mother's love is something
That cannot fully be defined or explained
A mother's love is far beyond defining
And it defies all explanation
A mother's love is God's design and not man's
A mother's love is real
A mother's love is special
A mother's love is unconditional
A mother's love is totally amazing
God knew exactly what we needed
When He created mothers
A mother's love is a love that is always there
A mother's love touches the heart
And leaves a footprint in the mind
A mother's love is a deep and abiding love
A mother's love endures all things
Nothing can destroy a mother's love
A mother's love is caring
A mother's love embraces
A mother's love is forgiving
A mother's love is nurturing
A mother's love is patient

A mother's love reveals that she is our best friend
When God created mothers
He knew what He was doing
A mother's love is there when it is needed most
A mother's love recognizes when there is hurt
A mother's love understands the struggles
A mother's love calms the fears
A mother's love never fails or falters
A mother's love is full of faith
A mother's love shares our joy, feels our pain
And embraces our dreams
A mother's love is forever strong
A mother's love will not allow a good mother to fail
In her God-given assignment
God needed mothers to play an important role
He gave mothers the tools and wisdom to be strong
God knew exactly what we needed
When He created mothers
And that is why
God gave us mothers and a mother's love

85

She Left a Legacy of Love

There is one word that adequately described her
And that word is love
Love defined her
Love inspired her
Love motivated her
And love is who she was
She loved God
She loved her family
And she loved life
She loved from the depths of her heart
She lived to love and love became her legacy
A legacy of love that affected
Generation after generation
And it was her legacy of love that she left behind
To those whom she loved
She left a legacy of love that was so strong
That it forever lives in the hearts and minds
Of those she touched
What she left was greater than an inheritance
Because what she left was a priceless
Unconditional love
She left a legacy of love that was strong
She didn't live her life to be remembered
But her life of love made her unforgettable
She was so many things to so many people
But most of all she was love
She was born to love
And loving others is what she did well
She didn't have riches and she didn't have fame
But what she did have was a lot of love to share
She left a legacy of love
It was her love
That made her an extraordinary woman
Her life left a great legacy of love

Her legacy of love became the chapters of her life
Her legacy of love revealed her amazing faith
Her legacy of love revealed a woman
Who believed in instilling high morals and values
In the many people she helped raise
Her legacy of love encouraged construction
Not destruction of life
Her legacy of love built up and nurtured
Her legacy of love revealed a woman
Who showed an inner strength
As she experienced life's hills and life's valleys
Her legacy of love left memories that will never die
Her legacy of love was the assurance
That when her life ended
The impact she had on those she loved
Would live on forever
She left a legacy in the hearts and minds
Of those she loved
That will never be forgotten
For she left a legacy of love

www.ingramcontent.com/pod-product-compliance
Lightning Source LLC
Chambersburg PA
CBHW021436080526
44588CB00009B/554